═══ In Praise of ═══
THE COURAGEOUS LIFE

"To live the courageous life you cannot tip-toe into the future. You must understand that life is not about safety. It is about growth. And you can only grow when you take on challenges—when you stretch yourself to be all that you can be, to do all that you can do, and have all the experiences that you can have. The fact that you are reading this book—*The Courageous Life*—means that you are now ready to take the next steps on your heroic path. Welcome to the club!**"**

—JACK CANFIELD, CO-CREATOR OF THE CHICKEN SOUP FOR THE SOUL SERIES
AND CO-AUTHOR OF *THE SUCCESS PRINCIPLES: HOW TO GET FROM
WHERE YOU ARE TO WHERE YOU WANT TO BE*

"Your dreams can come true! I fully believe this. *The Courageous Life* is an inspiring and practical new book that will help the reader clarify and then victoriously live out their dreams. I recommend it to anyone who feels compelled to courageously pursue a dream that has remained dormant for too many years.**"**

—DR. TOM HILL, EXECUTIVE COACH,
CO-AUTHOR OF *CHICKEN SOUP FOR THE ENTREPRENEUR'S SOUL*

"*The Courageous Life* both challenged me and provided practical tools to help clarify and move me toward my dreams and goals. The book is extremely engaging and thought provoking—while always remaining practical. It honestly changed my life!**"**

—RUSSELL DAWS, VP OF BUSINESS GROWTH & MARKETING
PRINCIPLE AND EXECUTIVE VP OF SALES & MARKETING, ELYSIUM CAPITAL

"In *The Courageous Life,* Ron Brown does a superb job of putting together a specific guide to discover and live out our purpose, passions and dreams. It not only gives a detailed step by step process to follow; it also serves as a companion and reference along the way."

—Dr. R. Paul Walters, Hospital Chaplain, Counselor with emphasis in Marriage and Family Therapy

"*The Courageous Life* provides energizing motivation and instruction for clarifying one's primary life dreams, goals, and purpose. Then, by presenting a compilation of extensive research, the book presents an engaging, step by step process for life change that will lead one to living out their dearest dreams."

—Lou Walters, RN, Hospice

"*The Courageous Life* is a stimulating, practical book on getting focus in your life and taking action. I found the book both inspiring and practical."

—Russ Taylor, RE/MAX Realty Associates

"*The Courageous Life* is a very good book about living a life where we pursue our visions and dreams. I have read the words of this book over and over again, because all too often I am tempted to give up on myself. Too often I am temped by discouragement to stop moving forward. Ron Brown encourages me to continue dreaming—to continue growing. Through his humorous, yet challenging style of writing, he encourages me to clarify my dreams and then move out toward those dreams. He has helped me to live courageously."

—Patric Reusser, Theologian, Reformed Church of Switzerland

"This is a book about living courageously, from the finest and most consistent en-Courager I know.**"**

—GREGORY BOYER, PHD, MBA, MANAGING DIRECTOR, GLOBAL INNOVATIONS FOR FAIR TRADE

"*The Courageous Life* helped me clarify, and then make the necessary changes to live out my dream and passion. I have now realigned my life and career in a way that is leading me to the top! A life-changing book.**"**

—SCOTT OLTHOFF, CERTIFIED FINANCIAL COUNSELOR

"When I read *The Courageous Life* I was stopped in my tracks. It forced my to re-evaluate where my life was headed, and then guided me down a new path leading toward my ultimate calling in life. I highly recommend this book to anyone who wants to live a Courageous Life!**"**

—MICHAEL CHITWOOD, DIRECTOR, TEAM WORLD VISION

Praise for **Ron Brown**

"Ron Brown delivers! He is committed to improving you and your business. His personal coaching has kept me on the path of truth and integrity. He has shown me it's the only way to do life and do business. The rewards have been beyond my expectations in every aspect: personal, spiritual, and financial. Through his knowledge and wisdom, Ron has helped me to see the bad, focus on the good, and remain on the straight and narrow path to success.**"**

—JOHN BELL, COMMERCIAL PILOT

"Ron has been a big help to myself, my team, and my agency. I consider him a friend and one of the best listeners I know."

—Brent E Shunk, CLU, CLTC,_Managing Director, Northwestern Mutual Financial Network

"Working side by side with Ron as a coach, I have found him to be a great mentor as well. He has a sincere desire to see others succeed. His own sense of fulfillment is fueled by helping others grow."

—David Clute, Consultant

"I've observed Ron as a friend, colleague, mentor, and professional consultant. Ron has the ability to lend sound wisdom and insight while communicating an application in a very practical way. His intent isn't to press his leadership beliefs on you or your organization, but to help bring out the potential that already exists by unveiling truths of leadership and organizational cohesiveness that often go overlooked. Ron's investment in me as a leader and friend has been a great gift to me, both personally and professionally."

—Dan Chitwood, Lead Pastor

"Ron Brown is an insightful and innovator thinker. He excels at molding complex information and situations into clear, objective outcomes. His open and engaging style invites others to explore their potential in creative and stimulating ways. Ron's diverse background and experience brings a refreshing approach to today's leadership challenges."

—Kerry Hearns-Smith, Business Consultant

"I have found Ron Brown to be a man of integrity,
who listens very intently before offering advice.
He is always offering encouragement to others
by sharing 'Life's Expectations'.**"**

—Larry Teague, Organizational Consultant,
Jadetree Associates

"Ron is an excellent listener. He has a way of not only hearing
what a person is attempting to say, but is able to then provide
excellent guidance that will help the situation. He is non-
confrontive, yet directly challenges people to grow.**"**

—Chuck Foran, Director of Development,
Northwestern Mutual Financial Network

"Ron's coaching brought my sales effectiveness up several levels.
Free of internal political maneuvering and industry-bias,
Ron helped me find key opportunities for growth."

—Sergio Murer, Senior Mortgage Broker

"Every time I meet with Ron, I come away with practical
insights that I can immediately put to use. Ron listens carefully,
asks perceptive questions, and has a knack for discerning
the underlying cause from the presenting symptoms.
He speaks with refreshing candor and conviction.
Simply put, he prompts me to grow."

—Brent Reese, Administrative Pastor

THE COURAGEOUS LIFE

RON BROWN, PhD

Foreword by **Jack Canfield**, co-creator
of the Chicken Soup for the Soul series

DreamTime Publishing, Inc.

DreamTime Publishing, Inc., books are available at special quantity discounts for bulk purchases for sales promotions, premiums, fund-raising, and educational needs. Please contact us at **www.DreamTimePublishing.com** for additional information.

Library of Congress Cataloging-in-Publication Data

Brown, Ron, Ph. D.
    The courageous life / Ron Brown ; foreword by Jack Canfield.
        p. cm.
    ISBN 978-1-60166-015-2 (hard cover)
    1. Success. 2. Courage. I. Title.
    BJ1611.2.B75   2008
    158.1—dc22

                                                                2008019760

Branding, website, and cover design for DreamTime Publishing by
    Rearden Killion • www.reardenkillion.com
Manuscript consulting by Jeannette Cézanne • www.customline.com
Text layout and design by Gary A. Rosenberg • www.garyarosenberg.com

This publication is designed to provide accurate and authoritative information in regard to the subject matter covered. It is sold with the understanding that the publisher is not engaged in rendering legal, accounting, or other professional service. If legal advice or other expert assistance is required, the services of a competent professional person should be sought.

    —From a declaration of principles jointly adopted by a committee of the
    American Bar Association and a committee of publishers.

This book is printed on recycled, acid-free paper containing
a minimum of 50% recycled, de-inked fiber.

Contents

*This book is dedicated
to my dearly loved wife, Martha,
my fellow dreamer of courageous dreams.*

Thank You

As with any courageous journey, there are special people who contributed to what is written in the following pages. Individuals who provided love, guidance, and support—and thus helped author this book.

Martha, my wife and best friend, is a constant encouragement and wholeheartedly supports my desire to write and see my dreams realized. This book could not have been written without her. In addition, my children, Austin, Calvin, and Taylor, have encouraged me along the way, providing patience and understanding as I took time to write.

My parents, Paul and Lou Walters, are two of my biggest fans and have always been there to provide love and counsel. They always believe in me. My father, Tom, and two brothers, Bruce and Doug, are comrades who I deeply love and appreciate.

There is also a group of personal friends, advisors, and mentors who have greatly contributed to this project by providing encouragement, critical feedback, and empowering friendship. These people include: Russ & Georgianne Daws, Russ & Charlene Taylor, Greg Boyer, Michael Chitwood, Scott Othoff, John Bell, Brent Reese, Patric Reusser, Jack Canfield, and Tom Hill.

I also want to acknowledge my agent, Linda Langton of Langton International Agency. When I was searching for an agent to represent this book, she quickly embraced the vision and worked tirelessly in her representation of this work. I am very grateful for her help and wise counsel. I also thank Meg Bertini and her team at DreamTime Publishing for their significant contribution to this book.

Finally, I thank God, who continually maintains a posture of love and grace toward me, my family, and our dreams.

Ron Brown
Mahomet, Illinois
May 2008

Foreword

"This is the true joy—the being used for
a purpose recognized as a mighty one."
—George Bernard Shaw

I believe every one of us was created with an inborn purpose—some special quality we have come to express into the world. For some—like Mother Teresa, the Dalai Lama, and Bishop Desmond Tutu—it may be love. For some others—like Martin Luther King, Jr., Bobby Kennedy, and Gandhi—it may be social justice. For still others—like Lance Armstrong, astronaut Neil Armstrong, and blind mountain climber Erik Weihenmayer—it may be courage.

No matter what it is, we have all come to bring that gift to the rest of humanity. One of the primary tasks for living a courageous life, a life that matters, a life that transcends the boring humdrum life that so many of us have unconsciously settled for, is to discover, accept, and honor your unique purpose. This book is a wake-up call. It is a call from Central Command to wake up out of the cultural trance that most of us live in and fulfill your destiny.

Fortunately, early in my career, I attended a weekend workshop in which one of the exercises was designed to help us clarify our life purpose. I discovered that the qualities I had come to explore and express were love and joy. We all have unique qualities that we are being asked to bring forward. It's as if each of us is a cell in a giant body called mankind. When we don't step up to the plate and fully embody our purpose, it is as if we are a diseased cell in that body. The whole of humanity suffers for the lack of our contribution.

Several years later, in another workshop, we were asked to focus more clearly on how we were going to express our purpose in our lives. When I looked to where I had experienced the most joy in my life, it was when I was teaching. I started out as a high school teacher in an inner-city high school in Chicago, later became a teacher trainer, a college instructor, a therapist, a trainer, and finally an author and professional speaker. My life purpose as I came to understand it is *to inspire and empower people to live their highest vision in a context of love and joy.* Everything I now do is in alignment with this purpose—the *Chicken Soup for the Soul* books that inspire people, my books on the principles of success that empower people by giving them the necessary tools they need, my seminars, and my coaching programs. Because of this, my life has been one of harmony, inner peace, joy, and outrageous success.

Without a clear understanding of your life purpose, you are most likely going to live a life of aimless drifting or allow yourself to be manipulated by the needs of others rather than be guided by your own inner compass. All too often the result is resignation, resentment, lack of enthusiasm and passion, and even depression. On the other hand, if you become aware of your true inner calling, your passions, and your most heartfelt desires—and have the courage to pursue them—your life can indeed become a magical, meaningful, heroic journey.

Once you truly understand and accept why you are here, you will become more deeply aware of your deepest, most heartfelt dreams and aspirations. Once you are connected to your purpose and dreams, and have the belief that you have the right, the ability, and the responsibility to pursue and achieve them, you will be asked to take the actions that will bring them into manifestation. For most of us, that takes a leap of faith. It can be scary. It takes commitment, courage, and persistence. It takes being willing to risk leaving the comfort of the familiar—even though the familiar may not be very satisfying—and to step out into the unknown. But what I and everyone else who has chosen to pursue their dreams has found is that all the things you want—all the good stuff—lies on the other side of fear. Daniel had to go into the lions' den, David had to face Goliath, Luke Skywalker had to face Darth Vader, and you will have to face your own demons, slay your own dragons. Fortunately, the dragons and beasts of mythology are only metaphors for your inner dragons that we must slay—your fear, your lack of self-confidence, your lack of discipline, your lack of self-awareness.

Every real, fictional, and mythical hero has had to face his or her fears and leave the comfort of home and face the unknown in order to fulfill his or her heroic destiny. Whether it is in the arena of war, business, sports, medicine, government, the creative arts, or simply being a good parent, to be effective we all have to become warriors. We have to act despite our fears, following our higher calling. Sometimes that higher calling asks us to risk our lives for our fellow man. Sometimes it requires us to risk our job or our friendships in the name of integrity. Sometimes it requires us to risk our unexamined beliefs and assumptions in the name of truth. The challenge can be as simple as overcoming the fear of sharing your true emotions with your friends and family or as profound as overcoming the fear of running for public office or the fear of jumping out of an airplane at ten thousand feet.

Fear is the most paralyzing of all human emotions. Fear stops us from trying, from daring, and ultimately from succeeding. Therefore fear must be courageously confronted so we never have to say, "I wish I had. I should have. Why didn't I?" As my good friend, self-made millionaire, radio and TV personality Bob Proctor has often stated, "We come this way but once. We can either tiptoe through life and hope that we get to death without being too badly bruised or we can live a full, complete life achieving our goals and realizing our wildest dreams."

To live the courageous life you cannot tiptoe into the future. You must understand that life is not about safety. It is about growth. And you can only grow when you take on challenges—when you stretch yourself to be all that you can be, to do all that you can do, and have all the experiences that you can have.

The path to the summit will not always be smooth, and the climb will not always be easy, but if you answer the call and accept the challenge to step through your fears and surmount the obstacles on the path, you will join an elite club of those who, throughout history, have successfully embraced their heroic calling. You have the choice, as you read this book, to embrace the magnificent being that you truly are and create the life of your dreams. And the best part is that once you start acting in alignment with your true purpose, the path becomes easier, the obstacles disappear more quickly, and all of the resources and support you need appear more easily.

There is a saying among the great traditions of the world, "When the student is ready, the teacher appears." The fact that you are reading this book—*The Courageous Life*—means that you are now ready to take the next steps on your heroic path. Welcome to the club! I look forward to seeing you at the top of the mountain!

—Jack Canfield
Cocreator of the Chicken Soup for the Soul series
and author of *The Success Principles: How to Get
from Where You Are to Where You Want to Be*

THE
COURAGEOUS
LIFE

CHAPTER 1

I Have a Dream...

*"The future belongs to those who
believe in the beauty of their dreams."*
—Eleanor Roosevelt

You have goals, visions, and dreams for your life. Even if you don't have them now, you had them in the past: passions and mental images of what you hope, or had hoped, to accomplish with your life.

While some people live out their dreams, many individuals eventually come to a point where they feel the need to release the dreams and goals they once had for their lives. Like a helium balloon that becomes untied from around the wrist of a little child, these people reach a point where they feel compelled to simply watch their dreams fade away into the foggy mist, forever lost, though never quite forgotten in their minds and hearts.

There are many reasons why people may choose to let go of their dreams, but in most cases their dreams simply get lost, buried under all the activities and rituals of daily life. Then, as they feel themselves getting older, as they sense life starting to slip away, these individuals begin to lose hope that the specific plans they once held so dearly can be accomplished at all. They wake up one day and start to wonder if they have lost their "window of opportunity" to really live life.

Maybe you can relate to this experience. If so, you are not alone.

A friend of mine shared the tragic story of a person with whom he'd graduated high school twenty years earlier. This individual was a star athlete and had the privilege of being one of the most popular students in his senior graduating class. He enjoyed the respect, friendship, and admiration of both his teachers and fellow students. While in college, his handsome appearance allowed him to earn extra income as a model, and though not recruited, he also walked on (and made) the University of Alabama football team under legendary coach Paul "Bear" Bryant. From his perspective, and of all those who knew him, his life was on track to be both fulfilling and successful.

But years later, after struggling through some addictions, he lost his marriage and family. In an attempt to restart his life, he moved out to California, where for a time his future seemed promising. But after a few short years, he reached a point of final hopelessness and quietly decided to take his own life. Before committing suicide, he wrote a simple note that read, "I can no longer live with the knowledge of who I am versus the knowledge of what I know I was capable of being."

There are too many men and women in this world who, in some way, sadly relate to what this man wrote in his good-bye message to the world. Like him, they feel a deep sense of loss and regret over what might have been. They live with a growing sense of regret over what should or could have been realized in their careers, families, friendships, and spiritual lives. And as these people approach midlife, they start to wonder if it is just too late to become all that they were created to be. Too late to live a life that reflects their deepest dreams, priorities, values, and desires.

One of the most famous speeches to seize the hearts and minds of people was the passionate discourse given by Martin Luther King, Jr. Delivered on the steps of the Lincoln Memorial in Washington DC on August 28, 1963, his speech captured the minds of young and old alike with a compelling vision. A vision, not of what *might* have been, but of *what still could be*. Though Dr. King's emphasis that day was a persuasive call for racial equality and unity, one reason his words strike a chord in almost everyone who has listened to that speech through the years is Dr. King repeatedly used a phrase that provokes an inner and heart response in every listener. That phrase is, "I have a dream."

On that hot summer day, standing under the majestic statue of Abraham Lincoln, Dr. King unveiled his personal dream to everyone present by saying:

> "I have a dream that one day this nation will rise up and live out the true meaning of its creed: 'We hold these truths to be self-evident: that all men are created equal.' I have a dream that one day on the red hills of Georgia the sons of former slaves and the sons of former slave owners will be able to sit down together at a table of brotherhood. I have a dream that one day even the state of Mississippi, a desert state, sweltering with the heat of injustice and oppression, will be transformed into an oasis of freedom and justice. I have a dream that my four children will one day live in a nation where they will not be judged by the color of their skin but by the content of their character. I have a dream today."

"I have a dream." This phrase touched everyone on that hot summer afternoon, and has continued to touch many more people through the years, because deep within our hearts we all have a dream. And to hear that great orator express his dream with such passion and conviction has prompted a compelling question in the minds of countless individuals. In addition to evoking thoughts regarding racial equality, that speech has sparked a compelling question we all need to answer—a question we all *want* to answer—which is: "What is *my* dream? If I had the chance to share my dream with anyone who would listen, what would it be? What would I say?"

Regretfully, many individuals cannot answer this fundamental question for themselves. They have either forgotten their dream or have lost faith in the dreams they once held so fondly for their lives. They have lost their dreams, and as a result can no longer clearly articulate their primary purposes in life. In addition, many people fear digging up and clarifying their dreams because they are afraid of being confronted with *what could have been.*

But I also believe most of these same people want help. They want help to once again draw out and re-clarify their dreams, passions, and visions. They desire encouragement and counsel so they can rediscover, understand, and articulate what their lives are to stand for and represent. It is the simple purpose of this book not only to guide you through the courageous process of clarifying the nature of your dreams, but also to put you on a path that will enable you to reach those dreams!

In his book *The Dream Giver,* Bruce Wilkinson writes that everyone is created with a dream or purpose that he or she is meant to accomplish in life. One may have forgotten this dream—may currently not be able to describe the dream—but deep down there is a dream inside each one of us.

Many of you sensed your unique dreams when you were much younger but have since forgotten or lost them underneath the demands of life. Your dreams have been covered up under the need to pay your bills, care for your children, attend church activities, change the oil in your car, visit the in-laws, and whatever it takes to maintain your livelihood. As a result, though you are able to check these activities off of your to-do list each week, you start to feel your life becoming quite ordinary. Driven by the constant onslaught of these never- ending duties, your life has drifted into a busy, yet mundane routine.

Until you discover (or rediscover) the underlying purpose for your life, you will continue to feel like you have missed the boat. You'll feel like you've missed your opportunity to be all you were created to be. Wilkinson, who launched Heart for Africa, which mobilized first-world volunteers to plant over five hundred thousand backyard gardens for orphans and the hungry, writes, "Tragically, a whole lifetime can pass without a person ever accomplishing the Great Thing that he or she was born to do and wants to do."

The good news is this does not need to be the case. There is hope! No matter your age or lot in life, you can clarify your unique purpose and reap the benefits and enjoyment of having lived out that specific purpose and dream in your life. This is what the "courageous life" is all about.

As I approached the age of forty, I sensed (or, to be honest, *knew*) that something was missing. I was starting my graduate work in organizational leadership when deep down I realized my life was not headed in a direction that excited me, a direction that would inevitably result in my life purpose being fulfilled. In fact, I did not even know what my life purpose was—let alone know how to get there. I now believe that I originally entered my graduate studies in search for some type of meaning in life. I was searching not only for significance but for the purpose of my existence.

In his book *The Greatest Miracle in the World,* Og Mandino wrote, "Most humans, in varying degrees, are already dead. In one way or another they have lost their dreams, their ambitions, and their desire for a better life. They have surrendered their fight for self-esteem and they have compromised their great potential." He adds that many people live inside prisons they have constructed with bricks fashioned from their own choices, habits, and behaviors. And after occupying these self-made prisons for a period of time, they start to believe they are incarcerated for life, when in fact they still possess the key that can set them free . . . if they will only use it. What these people need to realize is that their lives can be rebirthed. There are *simple* techniques a person can use to unlock their potential and get back on a path that will lead them toward their dreams.

This inner realization propelled me on a holy quest to not only clarify my purpose in life, but to do whatever it took to realign my life to that purpose. No more years were to be wasted just "doing" life. My remaining time would be spent living out my purpose and dreams. What I learned on this personal journey will be shared with you in the following pages. But let me start off with a word of encouragement: no matter what your age or lot in life, you too can arrive at a better understanding of your life purpose and dreams, and then experience the deep enjoyment and rewards of living them out.

At age thirty-four, Martin Luther King Jr. articulated his dream of racial equality and unity. Christopher Columbus set out to accomplish his vision of discovering a new trade route to the Orient at the age of forty-five, and found a new world in the process. At sixty, George Washington had a vision to provide needed leadership for a new nation, a government for the people and by the people. At the age of eighty, Moses received a vision to lead the Israelites to a new homeland. No matter what your age, you too can embark on a courageous journey toward the destination of your dreams.

In his best-selling book *The World Is Flat,* economist Thomas L. Friedman defines a measurement of societal and corporate health that applies to individuals as well. Friedman asks, "Does your society have more memories than dreams, or more dreams than memories?" He then makes this powerful statement: "When memories exceed dreams, the end is near."

No matter your age, or where you find yourself in life, you can discover your purpose and align your life to realize your unique dreams. It is possible. You do not have to live off the memories of yesteryear; you can set out on a journey leading to your dreams! It will not be easy, but be encouraged: many have gone before you in this heroic quest, and your example will provide encouragement for those who will follow. This quest will be part of your legacy, part of what you will be remembered for having become and achieved in life.

WHAT PREVENTS PEOPLE FROM LIVING OUT THEIR PURPOSES AND DREAMS?

Before getting started on how to specifically rediscover your dreams, you need to understand what *prevents* individuals from discovering and then living out their unique purpose and dreams. This is important because when you start to go through this process of rediscovery, at some point you will experience the same issues tugging at your life that distracted you from accomplishing your dreams in the first place.

This time, with new knowledge, things will be different. This time, you will have taken the time to discern what derailed you in the past, and this understanding will enable you to fight through the barriers that will inevitably arise as you once again reengage in the process of aligning your life to your dreams.

Author Frank Tyger writes, "Most barriers to your success are man-made. And most often, you're the man who made them." The issues we will review here are not insurmountable. None of them can, in the end, derail you from living out your dreams and passions—unless you allow them to do so.

In the past, some of these issues provided me with sufficient excuses to bury the dreams I had for my life. They provided enough resistance to make me question whether going after the vision I had for my life was worth it. But now, armed with a better understanding of these perceived giants, I am able to fight through these barriers as I reach out toward my future.

Sales guru Zig Ziglar writes that everyone is born into life with equal potential. But over a period of time, regardless of what has happened in your life (where you were born, who your parents are, your level of education, your economic status, or other circumstance), the day comes when you have to make the conscious choice to either let your past beat you . . . or teach you.

As you review these perceived barriers, be honest with yourself. Which ones have you allowed to derail you in the past? Which specific issues tempted you to make excuses and remain in the safety of your comfort zone? Which ones released you from the responsibility to strive toward the life you were created to live? Jesus said, "You shall know the truth, and the truth will set you free." Gandhi taught, "Truth quenches untruth." As you discover and admit the truth regarding what has prevented you from stepping out toward your dreams, you'll be set free to once again reach your true potential.

The major barriers I have found that prevent people from living out their purposes and dreams include a lack of faith, waiting for others to create one's future; false humility; lack of energy; lack of knowledge; fear; one's current level of security and contentment; and life itself. Let's review these one at a time.

1 Lack of faith

Faith can be defined as "being sure of what we hope for and certain of what we do not see." It includes having a profound belief or trust in a particular truth, future event, or unseen reality.

Deep down, many people do not believe they can change. Others doubt that pursuing their dream will be worth the effort. These individuals do not believe their current life can change very much for the better. They are no longer sure of what they hope for, nor certain of what they do not see.

In the past, efforts to lose weight, quit smoking, or control one's temper have resulted in small increments of positive change . . . only to be completely negated a month or two down the road during a holiday-season eating spree, a month of financial stress at home, or a confrontation with a cranky boss at work. Because of these past setbacks and defeats, we no longer believe we can sustain the changes needed to bring our dreams into reality.

U.S. Congressman (and author of many best-selling books on personal success) Bruce Barton writes, "Nothing splendid has ever been achieved except by those who dared believe that something inside them was superior to circumstance." If you do not believe you can change, you won't. But let me add this: if today, deep down, you honestly do not believe you can ever change, stay with me. Continue reading, because several years ago I also struggled with this same feeling. I felt stuck in a quasi-successful life, not quite sure if I had what it took to reshape my life into what I dreamed it could be.

Many people are uncomfortable with the whole concept of "faith." They pride themselves on being pragmatic thinkers with one foot set firmly in reality and the other set firmly in science. But those who live courageously have embraced the concept of faith, for faith is foundational to deep change. Faith allows us to be "sure of what we hope for and certain of what we do not see." It allows us to envision a new future for ourselves, and then enables us to reach that future. Author of the best-selling *The Traveler's Gift* Andy Andrews writes, "Reason never makes room for miracles. Reason can only stretch so far, but faith has no limits."

2 Waiting for others to do it for us

Some people spend their whole lives waiting for others to hand them their dream on some type of silver platter. They are waiting for the family inheritance to come through, to strike it rich in the lottery, to have their supervisor promote them at work, or maybe just waiting for someone to pick them out of the crowd. For many years I too sat around waiting for *my* opportunity to come my way. I figured if I was good enough, nice enough, smiled enough, was a person of noble character, then someone would eventually come along and hand me my dream.

Looking back, I now understand the foolishness of thinking that if I would just follow the rules, work hard, while waiting patiently off to the side, someone would eventually come and hand me my future. The frustrating thing was that while I was "patiently" waiting for my dreams to be handed to me, I noticed a small number of individuals, who at my age (and even younger) were *already* living out their dreams. They had already started their own business, sojourned to foreign lands, developed a strong financial portfolio, and accomplished other daring feats while maintaining a positive and joyful outlook on life. They were living their dreams, and even forming *new* dreams for their future. As I observed this select group of people around me, I knew I was missing something.

What I was missing was a clear understanding of my personal responsibility to choose and act on my own behalf. I was holding other people, not myself, responsible for fulfilling my vision.

Author and scientist Michael Kiefer writes that one of the natural laws that governs life is the "law of personal responsibility." Kiefer defines personal responsibility as "the act of holding oneself one hundred percent accountable for the circumstances for one's own life." This law states that you alone are personally responsible for how your life turns out, and that I am personally responsible for how my life turns out.

In fact, one common trait found in many world religions is that each person must one day stand before a divine entity and give account for their own life. We will not be able to make excuses, or transfer the blame to what our parents did or did not do. We will not be able to blame our boss for their ignorance of our special gifts and abilities. We will simply have to give account for our own choices and actions.

You have free will. You have the power to choose your way. You are not simply the victim of your workplace, culture, society, or upbringing, but have the power to choose what you do and what you pursue in life. "There is a choice you have to make in everything you do. So keep in the mind that in the end, the choice you make, makes you." (Anonymous)

You cannot wait for someone to hand you your dream. You are to move out yourself, many times by faith, into the unknown, away from your comfort zone and out toward your goals and visions. But always remember, you are never alone. Though others can not just "give" you your dreams, you can create a team of advisors and trusted friends who can guide and support you as you courageously step out toward your heroic dreams! More about that later.

3 False humility

This barrier relates to the one just mentioned. Some people do not want to appear as if they are promoting their own self-interests. They do not want to put personal desires for their own life before the needs of others. Thus they wait. In an effort to be "humble," they remain hesitant to actively and confidently pursue their own desires and passions.

Most perspectives of spiritual development call people to be humble, to walk in humility, to eschew self-aggrandizement. But there is also a false humility that prevents many people from taking initiative in their lives. True humility embraces your strengths, dreams, and opportunities while remaining sensitive to the needs of others in the process. You and I are responsible for our lives and future, and though humility should definitely mark your life while pursuing a dream, you should never relinquish your dreams in the name of humility, which allows you to simply ignore your responsibility to actively pursue your calling in life.

4 Lack of energy

Fatigue makes cowards of us all. In the research for their book, *The Power of Full Engagement,* Jim Loehr and Tony Schwartz found that managing one's energy, not one's time, was the key to high performance and personal renewal. They write, "The importance of physical energy seems obvious for athletes, construction workers, and farmers. Because the rest of us are evaluated by what we do with our minds rather than with our bodies, we tend to discount the role that physical energy plays in performance. In most jobs, the physical body has been completely cut off from the performance equation. In reality, physical energy is the *fundamental* source of fuel . . . It not only lies at the heart of alertness and vitality but also affects our ability to manage our emotions, sustain concentration, think creatively, and even maintain our commitment to whatever mission we are on."

Pursuing your dreams and passions takes energy and focused work. When a person's energy level is low, it will be very difficult for her to break out, pursue, and maintain the personal discipline needed to pursue a dream.

My brother owns a German shorthaired pointer who loves chasing and swimming after sticks, tennis balls, or whatever else is thrown into the lake we frequently visit in northern Minnesota. There is nothing like the joy in that dog's eyes, and the enthusiasm in his pant, as this pointer anticipates "the throw." And after a few fake tosses (you've all done this to a dog!) I toss a stick as far as my arm can muster. Then, like a bolt of lightning, off he goes, only to return a few minutes later with the stick in mouth, ready to do it all over again.

What I have discovered is that if I can keep that dog chasing sticks for a long enough period of time, the dog will eventually reach a state of fatigue where he is forced to quit. He just cannot continue. And if this dog reaches this level of fatigue, he is usually done—not just for a few minutes, but for the rest of the day. The dog will just lie there and sleep with the stick hanging out of its mouth for a long, long time.

Your body works in the same way. If your body is allowed to reach a certain level of fatigue, you end up being tired and worn out, not just for a few hours, but for a number of days. Therefore managing one's energy is a key factor to effectively pursuing a dream. Jim Loehr and Tony Schwartz write that "energy is the fundamental currency of high performance." In this go-go-go/action-packed world, you need to be careful that you take the time to manage your energy so you can maintain the fortitude and resilience needed to pursue a dream.

This involves keeping your life in balance. Balancing your need for rest and renewal with the need to work and execute well.

But there is a second and even deeper reason why fatigue can set into your life. This type of fatigue comes from the feeling that your life is off track. There is something about being off track in life that can bring a person into a state of weariness, a state of inner unrest. For example, when I feel that my marriage, spiritual life, physical-fitness routine, or other relationships are off track, my entire life will start to feel in a state of unrest.

Stephen Covey writes, "The truth is . . . we are all off track most of the time, all of us—every individual, family, organization or international flight to Rome. Just realizing this is a significant step. But for many of us, the feeling of being off track brings with it discouragement and despair. It needn't and shouldn't be so depressing. Knowing we're off track is really an invitation to realign ourselves with true north (principles) and recommit ourselves to our destination."

When I believe my marriage, spiritual life, physical life, and other areas are making good progress, when I feel my life is growing in these areas, I then feel invigorated and ready to attack the *other* areas of my life as well, including my dreams. This is because success breeds success.

5 Lack of knowledge

When a person feels he lacks sufficient knowledge or understanding regarding what it will take to accomplish a dream or goal it can be very de-motivating. The questions that fill his mind can paralyze him from taking steps into the unknown that will be required if he's going to pursue a new dream. Furthermore, pain felt from *past* experiences, when he went into a situation with insufficient knowledge, can also prevent him from confidently stepping out toward a new venture.

For example, I do not like to sail. I don't like sailboats and I don't like sail masts. I was about ten years old when our family bought a little sailboat called a Puffer. Though this name sounds innocent enough, it only covered up the real fact that if this Puffer caught the right amount of wind on a lake, the boat would suddenly develop a mind of its own and take off at tremendous speeds (at least from the perspective of a ten-year-old!) across the lake.

I remember taking the Puffer out for my first spin with my older brother as copilot. Things were going just fine until we rounded the bend of the lagoon and set sail toward the open lake. The slight breeze we had experienced in the lagoon suddenly turned into a mighty wind, and we were off to the races. The mast swung violently back and forth at head level while the Puffer tore out over the waves of the open and expansive sea (well, OK, it was really just a lake).

Now, initially this was all a bunch of fun. The wind was driving our little Puffer in a straight line across the lake, easy as can be . . . at least until we needed to change course and tack (whatever that meant) back to our side of the lake. This did not go very well. After a good forty-five minutes trying to maneuver the sail, paddling against the waves (the mast hitting my head several times), and doing whatever else we could think of to get back home, my father started yelling complex sailing instructions from the shore. As our dad tried to help, my brother and I just started to cry. Eventually our father just gave up, took off his shirt and swam out to us, climbed into that darn Puffer and, with *his* knowledge of sailing, quickly had us back to our dock.

I have not liked sailboats since that day.

Sometimes when I ponder taking up a new hobby or developing a new idea, a vivid picture of my experience in that Puffer enters my mind. My lack of control, lack of ability to tack (whatever that means) raises fears that I may fail in this *new* endeavor as well.

If you feel a lack of competence in one area of life, it may keep you from ever attempting to accomplish a dream in another area of life. In a few instances it may prevent you from taking an unwise risk, but too often you can allow a perceived lack of knowledge paralyze you from pursuing your courageous dreams. Instead, you talk yourself into playing it safe, rather than playing to win. Your fears win out.

 Fear of the unknown

Still trembling, Ordinary picked up his suitcase, turned his back on Familiar, and walked to the sign. And even though his fear kept growing, he shut his eyes and took a big step forward—right through the invisible Wall of Fear.

And there he made a surprising discovery.

On the other side of that single step—the exact one Ordinary didn't think he could take—he found that he had broken through his Comfort Zone.

—from *The Dream Giver*
by Bruce Wilkinson

Best-selling author and theologian John Ortberg writes, "My story, like every human story, is, at least in part, the struggle between faith and fear." Author of the *Rich Dad, Poor Dad* series, Robert Kiyosaki adds, "We all have tremendous potential and gifts. Yet, the one thing that holds all of us back in some degree is self-doubt . . . It is excessive fear and self-doubt that are the greatest detractors of personal genius."

Our fears can make cowards of us all. Fears *conquered* make heroes of us all.

I like to feel safe. I like to feel secure. Sometimes there is nothing as nice as feeling all warm and comfortable in my lounge chair watching a basketball game while eating a stack of chocolate chip cookies. But you know what, even though I *like* to feel safe and comfortable, it is also boring. If I sit too long in that chair, eating all those cookies, in time I start to feel tired and de-motivated. After a game or two, I feel sluggish and bored.

On the other hand, I don't like experiencing fear. I know it isn't a very profound realization, but it is true nevertheless . . . my fears scare me. But I have also discovered that on the other side of fear are feelings of energy, exhilaration, and passion.

Take skydiving. Talk about fear! A few years ago I went through a few hours of training one afternoon, was put on a plane, and after it finally reached a certain altitude, I was expected to jump out of it. I do not remember a more terrifying experience in my life. I remember sitting on the floor of an old single-prop plane waiting as it circled and circled, working hard to gain altitude. After we had reached about six thousand feet (which looked and felt like five *million* feet), my instructor proceeded to lie on the floor of the plane with his head sticking out the open door looking for a hole in the clouds for us to jump through. I remember thinking right after the instructor yelled, "Be ready to go on my signal!" that I was going to die. In fact, for some reason, I *knew* I was going to die.

Finally, after a few more minutes circling and looking for that hole in the clouds, the instructor yelled "Let's *go!*" and in the rush of it all I jumped out into the clouds filling the sky. That day, I jumped through my fears and experienced the exhilaration of falling through the sky— riding on the winds of the world, guided by a simple nylon parachute. It was one of the most exciting trips in my life.

Everything you want is on the other side of fear. Many of the most enriching experiences in life will follow a time when you choose to walk through a specific fear; yet some people will do almost anything to avoid their fears. As Jack Canfield writes, "All successful people have been willing to take a chance." They are willing to take a step of faith, trust their intuition, and simply "go for it" in life.

Many spiritual traditions and world myths tell stories of people overcoming fears, overcoming their inability to take chances. Fear is the primary reason why many individuals do not reach their potential or live out their dreams. Fear prevents one person from the commitment of marriage. For another, the fear of financial failure prevents them from starting their own business. And yet another person never makes a desired career change because they fear leaving the security of their current position. Fears paralyze your potential.

Whenever you "know" that you can't do something, it's time to reexamine that so-called knowledge. One principle of the Zen tradition is called "not-knowing," which enables a person to give up "fixed ideas about one's self and the universe." It's referring to fixed ideas that many times stand in the way of reaching your dreams.

Pursuing your dreams will always demand that you step through your fears. Your dreams will require you to take steps that lead you outside your comfort zone and into the unknown. You must be ready to courageously step through your fears so you can experience the exhilaration of falling through the sky all by yourself—riding on the winds of a dream.

7 Your present level of comfort & contentment

"Show me a thoroughly satisfied man,
and I will show you a failure."
—Thomas Edison

In *Good to Great*, author Jim Collins writes that "the enemy of becoming great is already being good." Put another way, if you are already somewhat satisfied with your current level of comfort, this feeling of comfort may be one of the biggest obstacles you must overcome when considering a new and exciting dream.

For example, our current level of financial security can prevent us from taking the financial risk to start a new business or impact the world by giving money to a social relief organization. Or, in my case, a current habit of taking an enjoyable vacation to Florida each summer can work to prevent our family from saving the money needed to take our dream vacation to Europe.

I love to spend a week or more each year on the beaches of Florida. My wife and kids always look forward to times when we can sit by the ocean, eat junk food, bodysurf, and listen to music. Our family has gone to Florida for many years and, quite frankly, we are very content with these relaxing excursions on the sandy shores of the Atlantic Ocean.

But you know what? I have a *dream* vacation. On this vacation, we would spend three weeks as a family traveling Europe, taking in the history, culture, food, and people who make Europe such an exciting place to visit. I envision starting off in Amsterdam and then traveling by rail through Germany into Austria, Hungary, and then back through Greece, Italy, and finish with visiting a good friend in Switzerland. We would stay in hostels, visit old cathedrals, and take in lunch or dinner at corner cafés.

I have been to Europe a few times by myself, but I really want to experience it with my family. I truly do. But I also like the beach in Florida, my family likes the beach, we are comfortable going to the beach, we know where to stay, park our van, and where we like to eat. It is familiar, easy, and good. And it is this present level of comfort and contentment that is preventing me from stepping off our well-beaten path twice a year to Florida onto a new path that will lead us to Europe, to what I honestly believe would be our best vacation ever.

Often your current level of comfort and contentment prevents you from stepping out toward something you know will be even more pleasurable and fulfilling. Your present level of pleasure, safety, and comfort lures you away from taking the risk of trying something new and better, and thus you miss the opportunity to grow, having become entrenched in the status quo.

The world is so convenient. Almost everything you want can be easily obtained on the Internet, bought at the local mall, restaurant, theater, or other venue.

Pursuing a dream is not convenient and it will always involve risk. Yet the choice is yours. You can choose to simply live a *good* life and go on *good* vacations—or you can step out and live a *great* life, go on *great* vacations, and experience a new world. The truth is, settling for a "good" life will leave you with too many regrets. But it is the choosing to live a great life that one finds joy and fulfillment.

8 Life itself

A last major barrier that prevents people from living out their unique purpose and dreams is . . . life itself. Bills, schedules, the needs of those you care about, health issues, and a list of other concerns can prevent you from taking the time to assess your life and ask the important questions: *What is my purpose? What is my dream? And how do I align my life to live out that purpose and dream?* In the end, life itself can easily derail you from pursuing your unique dreams and goals. Your daily routines can sap your energy, make you feel small, and easily keep you from taking time to discover a new path for your life.

We live in a society where our to-do list drives our daily activities. Bills need to be paid, the food pantry restocked, children's sporting events attended—the list just keeps getting longer and longer. Many people move along at an incredible speed, and though this speed allows them to get a lot of things checked off their to-do lists, there remains an eerie feeling that they are spending a lot of energy on things that, in the end, don't really matter. They have a lingering fear that this constant activity is only leading them further away from their heartfelt goals, dreams, and passions.

Author, pastor, and leadership expert Bill Hybels writes that "the most difficult person you will ever lead is yourself." And a primary task of leading oneself effectively is to manage this constant barrage of activity. Hybels writes that many of our lives are traveling at the speed of Mach Two (twice the speed of sound). And the question we need to honestly ask ourselves is what of enduring value can be richly experienced at a speed of Mach Two? What kind of relationships, love, care, forgiveness, and passion can be realized when we are traveling down the road of life at twice the speed of sound? The answer is obvious . . . not much.

So there you are—a list of the barriers that can prevent a person from living out their purpose and dreams. While this isn't a complete list, it's thorough enough to show that there are many obstacles that, if left unconquered, can keep you from successfully living the courageous life.

But be encouraged: with proper preparation, each one of these barriers can be overcome. This book will walk you through a plan to help you both successfully overcome these barriers and forever remain on a heroic path leading toward your dreams.

A popular song by Tom Petty is "Runnin' Down a Dream." And that is what this courageous journey is all about: it's about running down your dream. The courageous life is about pursuing with passion the mystery that lies within your heart, and courageously choosing to follow where it leads. So, again, stay encouraged and focused, for when you finally arrive at the summit of your dream, the joy you will experience will forever outweigh the price you had to pay along the way.

CHAPTER 2

If I Have a Dream...
What Is It?

Dreams.

Scientists say we experience dreams every night while sleeping. While most of these dreams are forgotten, a few of the movies that play in your mind during the middle of the night are vivid enough to be remembered into the next day.

Personally, I have a recurring dream where I am in junior high, standing in front of my locker, having totally forgotten the combination. The class bell is ringing and, in desperation, feeling pressure to not be late to class, I am turning the combination around and around trying to remember the three numbers that open the lock. It is then that I always wake up, feeling relieved—not only because it was just a dream, but relieved that my years in junior high have long since passed.

You and I were created to dream. I am constantly amazed how each night my inner conscious is continuously creating movies that get shown on the inner screen of my mind during the wee hours of the night. It is quite amazing. Even while you are awake doing some mundane task during the day, or sitting through a boring business meeting, your mind will many times drift away and envision exciting possibilities for this world, and your own life. Your thoughts will naturally start to create rolling pictures of some new product you could invent, a deeper relationship you could nourish, or new career you could venture out and try.

Sometimes while driving my Jeep down a long stretch of highway, my thoughts will naturally start to float off and dream. Sometimes these thoughts envision quitting my current job and buying a small cottage on some Caribbean island where each day I can sit by the ocean and listen to music while I read and write various articles and books.

This picture is burned vividly into my mind. The cottage where I live is white, has a front porch shaded by palm trees, and faces the sunrise about three hundred feet from the shoreline. My mornings are spent thinking and writing. Evenings are spent with good friends at some beachside café . . .

But then it always happens. My car hits some pothole, or I see a police officer, and my mind quickly swings back into my current life. Back in reality, driving my Jeep on an interstate through the flat farmlands of central Illinois.

But do you know what? Despite that pothole, my Caribbean dream still remains, and I am not ashamed of it. Though I may be driving on some long stretch of highway today, I believe that someday I will have that quiet cottage on some white sandy beach somewhere. This is one of my dreams, and one I fully believe can happen with proper planning and determination. So my question to you is, *What are your dreams? Where does your mind naturally go when it has the freedom to soar?* Mark Twain wrote, "Twenty years from now you will be more disappointed by the things you didn't do than by the ones you did. So throw off the bowlines. Sail away from the safe harbor. Explore. Dream. Discover."

What are your dreams? What do you want to discover in life? Where do you want to explore?

The challenge of this book is to start on your courageous journey *now*. To start *now* clarifying, and pursuing, the dreams that have been placed in your heart. Individuals who are happy, successful, and fulfilled are those who are pursuing and living out their dreams. They are not waiting. They get up each day and proactively make choices that will move them down a pathway, possibly through the unknown, toward their personal goals and passions. They are acting *now.* They are living courageously. My hope is that this book will embolden you to do the same.

Your first step in taking this journey is to clarify what your dreams are. This will not be easy, and it will take time to uncover the specific goals and dreams that lie deep within your heart. But it can be done. So before we venture too far, let's clarify in more detail what a dream is.

WHAT IS A DREAM?

A dream is simply a burning picture in your heart and mind of what you deeply and definitively want your life to be guided by, stand for, and accomplish. It is the mental picture of what you want your life to reflect as a spouse, parent, friend, and human being.

What you are reading right now are the words that make up my first book. For many years, I had a personal dream to write a book. Through the years, many people have encouraged me to write, but I kept putting it off—until now. So in these pages, you are witness to one of *my* dreams being fulfilled. To write! And, more specifically, to write a book that helps others live a healthy and balanced life while enabling them to take specific steps toward their personal potential. This book is not the only dream I have for my life, but it is one specific dream I have had for a long time.

So again, my question to you is, What are *your* dreams? Where do *your* thoughts naturally take you to when they are given the freedom to drift and create your future?

Your dreams will take time to uncover, name, and clarify. This is to be expected, so be patient in the process. Just as a fine wine gets better over time, you will need to be patient and allow your dreams and passions to ferment and mature over time as well. This process will include the very important task of formulating your overarching life dream, which I will refer to as your personal life-mission statement. Clarifying your life-mission statement will be discussed in more detail in chapter five but a few thoughts regarding this statement are in order here because it will provide the foundation from which your list of specific dreams will later be created.

Your life mission can also be called your overarching life dream, and it states in very simple terms what you want your life to stand for. It defines who you want to be.

Clarifying and writing my personal life-mission statement took a few months to complete. Using a process similar to what will be described later, I started by writing a straightforward statement intended to help me define what I wanted the focus of my life (in general) to stand for. That first statement was then revised and rewritten, and with each new revision, I knew I was getting more clarity. But I also felt aggravated because the process was taking longer than expected because I had difficulty clarifying, in just a few sentences, the passions that resided deep within my heart. But then one day it happened. As I finished making a few tweaks to some words, I knew I had it. Before me was the "life-mission statement," which defined the overarching purpose for my life.

Over the next few months, this initial statement was revised and revised until finally all my work synergized into a simple statement that reflected my passions and life calling. It was a clear description of what I wanted my life to be about, and this statement has not changed since that day. Today, my life-mission statement reads:

"To reach, and mentor others to reach, our highest God-given potential while living a balanced life."

From this statement I then created specific short-term and long-term dreams to help me pursue this life mission. Remember, I have a number of "dreams" that I want to accomplish in my life (like my dream to write this book), but they all flow intimately out of my overarching life mission.

To get started on your courageous journey, your first step is to spend time creating the *first* draft of your own life-mission statement. To help you do this, the following is a list of questions for you to ponder, reflect upon, and then clarify in writing with the help of a journal. Take a couple of hours and go off to some beach, park, or quiet corner restaurant booth and dig deep into your heart and write down your thoughts to the following questions. (There are also journal pages provided in the back of this book.)

* When am I most naturally myself? What people, places, and activities allow me to feel most fully myself?

* What is my greatest talent? What have I always been good at doing?

* What do I love to do? How can I get paid for doing what I love to do?

* Who are my most inspiring role models? Why is this so?

* How do I enjoy being of service to others?

* What is my heart's deepest desire?

* What needs do I care about the most?

* What makes me feel most fulfilled?

* What have I felt called to do?

* What legacy would I like to leave?

As you ponder these questions, write a first draft of what your overarching life-mission statement (or overarching life dream) *might* be. In addition, make an initial list of specific dreams and goals that energize you and support the fulfillment of your life mission.

So go ahead and create a first draft of your life-mission statement and initial list of dreams, while remembering this critical thought: *do not talk yourself out of any vision or dream that enters your mind.* Be bold and allow your thoughts to flow honestly and freely in your mind and then into your journal. Remember that a courageous life starts with courageous dreams!

Later in this book you will be guided through a process to further clarify your life mission and list of dreams, but your first step is simply to take some time and ponder the questions listed above and record your initial thoughts, dreams, and desires. Jack Canfield writes, "One of the main reasons why most people do not get what they want is that they have not decided what they want." My challenge for you is to take time to decide what you really want your life to stand for and accomplish.

As you start, let's review four guiding principles to assist you in this process:

1 Your dreams are uniquely yours

The first guiding principle is that your dreams will be uniquely yours . . . and nobody else's. For example, I have a friend whose dream is to work on a NASCAR pit crew. While this is the last thing I want to do with my life, it is a very real and passionate desire for him. There is another friend who wants to be a sports announcer, and he is focused and working hard to make his dream a reality. Another wants to own his own charter plane company, and yet another wants to become an actress. And my list could go on.

The point is that your dreams are unique. While there may be others who have similar desires and passions, there will always be something about your dream that will make it unique, and thus truly yours alone. This is important for us to understand, because if your dreams are unique, there is a good chance that others may look at your dream and think it is foolish or unrealistic. And you need to prepare yourself for this response.

There will always be certain individuals who will not understand why you would want to pursue your dream. It is like my friend who wants to work on a NASCAR pit crew. Personally, banging my knuckles on car engines, working fifteen or more hours a day during the racing season, and changing tires in ten seconds or less is not even close to my dream job—but it *is* a dream job for my friend. So I tell him to go for it!

If your dream is unique, then there is a good chance you will be the only one who will fully understand it. Others may try, but only you (and *possibly* a few others) will fully believe in, and understand, your desires and passions. After graduating with a degree in electrical engineering, I worked as an engineer for a local electric utility company. While I enjoyed my work, I also sensed within myself a growing desire to leave my engineering career and join a ministry that worked with local teenagers.

I had already volunteered for this youth ministry for several years, and was feeling the desire to do it on a full-time basis. To some of my family and friends, pursuing this dream was an illogical and unwise decision. Why would anyone leave a high-paying electrical engineering career to work with teenagers, where I would make only forty percent of my current income! Why would anyone want to leave such a secure future for the uncertainty of working in a ministry where salaries were entirely dependent on consistent financial contributions from individuals and organizations within the community? Though others may not have understood such a choice, I did. I understood my choice, because the dream was mine.

Don't get me wrong, this decision was very difficult because it involved a lot of risk and required that I step through many fears in the process. But after spending about one year contemplating this choice, I made the decision to go for it. I made a change of careers and have never once regretted it. Though I enjoyed my work as an engineer, I have never regretted the choice to follow my passions and dream. In the end, I worked full-time in that ministry for sixteen years, filling a variety of roles, and continue to serve today in a part-time capacity.

Your dreams are unique to you. Allow them to be so. Do not expect others to fully understand your dreams, or your choice to follow those dreams. This is OK. And though others can be extremely helpful as we pursue a dream, in the end your dreams are yours, and yours alone.

2 Your dreams are already in you

A Small Boy

A small boy looked at a star and began to weep.
The star said, "Boy, why are you weeping?"
And the boy said, "You are so far away.
I will never be able to touch you."
And the star answered, "Boy, if I were not
already in your heart, you would not be able to see me."

—John Magliola

Another guiding principle you need to understand as you enter into this process is that your dreams are *already* in you. For most of you, your dreams just need to be once again uncovered and re-clarified. Best-selling author Bruce Wilkinson writes, "Like a genetic code that describes your unique passions and abilities, your Big Dream has been woven into your being from birth . . . And you have it for a reason: to draw you toward the kind of life you were born to love!"

Your dreams *already* lie within you. As mentioned earlier, sometimes they will make their way to the surface of your thoughts while you are driving on some long stretch of highway, or sitting under a tree in a park.

It is during times like these that your heart will remind you of the dreams that already lie deep within you. And so the hard work of pursuing your courageous dreams is not in creating a *new* dream, but in rediscovering the dreams that *already* lie deep within your heart. You just need to be honest with yourself and carefully uncover that which has been there all along, residing in the corners of your soul.

There is a war raging for your dreams. There is a war being fought between who you were created to be versus your tendency to conform to the demands of the world. Bruce Springsteen in his song "Blood Brothers" laments that people easily lose themselves in the tedious everyday requirements of life, of work, of bills that must be paid.

You must never give into what Springsteen calls the "hardness of this world." You can never let your dreams simply drift away, but must continually fight to breathe new life into the dreams and passions that stir in your soul.

For many years I dreamed about getting my doctoral degree in theology, human behavior, or leadership. But as I focused on an engineering career, and then later on my ministry work, this dream got buried under my "work to do and bills to pay." But through the years this dream remained, resurfacing in my mind while I was driving (again) on some long-forgotten road, listening to some boring speaker, or sitting by the beach listening to the surf roll in. But it was also a dream I kept trying to bury—for how could I afford the $15,000/year tuition for such a program? How could I hold down a full-time job while also committing to the rigors of graduate school? I just did not see how this dream could be actually realized.

Finally, after years of trying to suppress the desire to get my doctorate, I decided to breathe life into this old dream to see what could happen. I started researching various graduate schools, thinking through possible financial options, and assessing how I could restructure my life to handle the additional academic load. As I took steps toward my dream, I slowly found myself starting to believe that this dream *could* be realized. I started to reject my old belief that the costs and time necessary to complete such a program were too significant to overcome. I breathed life into my dream, and about five years later, my family and I traveled to Virginia Beach where we all celebrated as I walked across the stage to receive my PhD in organizational leadership, with my degree completely paid for!

Take courage. Your dreams are already in you. And where are they? Well, they are right where you buried them a long time ago. This leads us to the third, yet related characteristic, which will mark your dreams.

3 Your dreams will always remind you that they are there

Where does your mind drift when you are sitting at the seaside watching the surf? Where do your thoughts go when you are relaxed, sitting on a porch swing, gazing at the stars on a warm summer night? What dreams swell up inside of you when your thoughts are free to sail?

Your dreams will always look for opportunities to flow into your conscious thoughts. Though they may have been suppressed for many years, they are always lurking beneath the surface, ready to reenter your conscious mind when given permission to do so.

I grew up in an artistic family. My mother is a painter and musician, and creative in many other ways as well. In grade school, I would sit in my bedroom and spend hours drawing picture after picture of race cars and fighter jets, and after just a few years I had boxes full of the pictures drawn during my many hours spent with paper, magic markers, and colored pencils. But later, while in middle school, I made new friends and became active in football, basketball, track (though I hated to run), drama, choir, and other activities. Then I went off to college, earned an engineering degree, and proceeded to pour myself into my various careers.

Many years have passed since I spent those hours drawing fighter jets and race cars in my bedroom. But now, once again, in my mid-forties, I find myself being naturally drawn back into the arts. For example, my wife is an interior decorator, and whenever she is working on a project for a client, I enjoy helping her in the design work. And the interesting thing is that she likes many of my ideas!

This is just one small example of how your dreams and passions will continually seek to work their way back onto the surface of your lives, all through your lives. We may bury them under layers of time and life, but they will always be there, knocking at the door, ready to resurface in your mind when given the chance.

One reason some people drift into a depression during midlife is because they reach a point where they suddenly realize the dreams they once had when they were younger, dreams that were ignored during the years they built their families and careers . . . are *still* there. Now, later in life, their dreams have resurfaced in subtle ways, and they simply do not know what to do. They feel trapped in their current life, and as a result of this inner tension, they start to drift into a slight (or even deep) depression. They know there is a preferred life to be lived, but feel ensnared in their current reality and comfort zone. Yet all the while, their dreams keep reminding them that they are there—ready, if only allowed, to reinvigorate their lives.

Be honest with yourself. What are your inner thoughts and desires saying to you? Start clearing off the layers of dust and discern what these courageous voices are trying to say. Allow your dreams to surface into your conscious mind and then record them in your journal.

4 In some form, your dreams are realistic and doable

So your dream is to be the president of the United States. Is this an example of a courageous and realistic dream—or is it just a foolish fantasy?

So you want to own your own restaurant business, play bass guitar in a country band, or possibly sell your business and buy a charter fishing boat in Florida. Are these more realistic goals when compared with someone's dream to be president, or are they still unrealistic fantasies that ignore the realities of life?

At first, many of your dreams will seem crazy and unrealistic. This is a common and natural feeling that many people experience when they start to clarify their heart's desires. Your *present* life and circumstances will make many of your emerging dreams appear difficult to accomplish and quite unrealistic. The self-imposed limits of your current lives will make any thought of venturing out in a new direction seem ludicrous, and your current comfort zone will do all it can to prevent us from taking your dreams seriously. That's why pursuing a dream is such a heroic calling. Remember, the heroes who have gone before you in this quest felt many of these same feelings; they just chose to step through those fears. And you are being challenged to do the same.

So what about the dream to become president of the United States? Is this a realistic expectation, or just crazy fantasy? I will guarantee you this—this dream is not foolish. It is this kind of courageous dream that not only helped birth this nation, but has sustained it for over 225 years.

The real issue is not whether your dreams are "realistic," but whether we have the courage and fortitude to indeed step out and walk down a road that may, or may not, lead to that dream being realized. Whether or not you become the president is only of secondary importance. What matters is who you are forced to *become* as you walk down that road. What matters is how you will be transformed as you take specific steps in the direction of your courageous dreams and goals. Business philosopher Jim Rohn writes, "The ultimate reason for setting goals is to entice you to become the person it takes to achieve them."

As you step out toward your dream to be president, you will either eventually become the president, or you will have no regrets that you tried. As you sail away from your "comfort zone" onto the open sea, your dream will be refined, strengthened, and clarified by the wind, surf, and tides of life. And in this process, one of three things will happen. You will either some day win the presidential election, or you will have no regrets trying, or, third, in the process have your dream re-clarified in ways that would never had occurred if you had not taken the risk to step out and pursue what you originally thought was your life passion.

The fact is, you are a very poor judge of how realistic your dreams are. This is because whenever you ponder venturing out into the unknown, your fears will be right there trying to convince you to play it safe. You counter these fears by remembering that your dreams, coupled with active faith, can bring almost any "impossibility" into reality. History is full of such stories. Full of real-life stories that support a central truth that with faith "*all* things are possible." Whether you want to move mountains, or start your own business, your dreams coupled with active faith can produce amazing results.

Step out! Don't play it safe. Be bold. You have everything to gain when you courageously step into your future. A friend once told me, "Lewis and Clark did not start out with a map, but they came back with one." Sometimes you will not have your path completely mapped out before you start on your courageous journey into the future, but my challenge for you is to be determined and set out. One day you will come back with a map for others to follow as you mentor them in their own quest toward a dream.

Though your dreams will be further clarified and refined as you progress toward them, trust your inner desires—for they are in your heart for a reason and thus, in some unique form, are realistic and attainable.

ALWAYS REMEMBER, SOMEDAY YOUR LIFE WILL END

The fundamental reason you need make this courageous choice to step out, risk, and pursue your dreams is that, on your deathbed, I believe you will look back and evaluate your life based on three specific criteria. You will reflect back and evaluate your life on whether you:

1. Lived a life that focused on pursuing your unique dreams, goals, and passions.

2. Did so while maintaining healthy relationships with family, friends, and others.

3. Are adequately prepared for the life that follows this one, should that be your belief.

The reason you need to stay focused on the hard work of pursuing your dreams is that when you approach the end of your life, you won't care whether you owned season tickets to your favorite sport teams; it won't matter if you drove a BMW, Mercedes, or other luxury car, and the size of the house you lived in will seem inconsequential. In the end, what will matter is how you lived your life.

And a major criterion will be whether you made an honest and concentrated attempt to reach your potential and live out your unique dreams. I am quite confident that those who have already gone before us would testify to this fact.

Dr. Robert Clinton, once a professor of leadership at Fuller Seminary, researched leaders and noted six reasons why some leaders fail in their leadership, and it applies equally well to persons of all faiths. The six reasons why leaders do not finish strong are:

1. They lose their learning posture in life.

2. The attractiveness of their character wanes (people like to be with them less and less).

3. They stop living by their convictions. They have them, teach them, but no longer center their lives around them.

4. They are not investing themselves in lasting and eternal actions.

5. They stop walking in an awareness of their influence and destiny. They lose focus on the work they once felt inspired to do.

6. They lose their once-vibrant relationship with their Creator.

These same warnings apply to you and me. Though the work of pursuing your dreams will be difficult, losing focus on this task will lead to greater regret. Burying your dreams, or ignoring their significance, puts you on an immediate path toward a premature "internal" death, for if left unattended, your inner life can start to wither and die many years prior to when you physically die.

My decision to leave a career in electrical engineering to enter the ministry took over two years to make, but what sealed the deal was this simple thought: I did not want to live my life with any regrets. At the end of my life, I did not want to look back and wonder if I should have taken that leap of faith and tried a career choice that, for whatever reason, kept bubbling up inside of my soul. All during those months when I was trying to decide what to do, the desire to enter ministry would not fade away—even though my fears kept trying to drive that desire deep underground.

I recall later describing to a friend what helped solidify my choice to change careers. My own tradition, as you have no doubt guessed by now, is Christian; and I told my friend that when my life was over and I was standing before God, I would rather hear Him say, "Ron, I really did *not* want you to go into ministry, but hey, thanks for giving it a try," than hear God say, "Ron, for over two years I was prompting you into a life that I knew would deeply satisfy you in every way. I know you felt my tug. But for some reason you allowed your fears to keep you from experiencing that life and those blessings. I still blessed your life, but I was also looking forward to using you in ministry in a mighty way."

The choice is yours. Either choose to bury your dreams and potential, and experience the regret of doing so—or choose to be your own hero and venture out, take risks, and walk through your fears toward your calling and dreams. The second choice will be more difficult than the first, and the pain along the way will be even more real, but the reward of reaching the summit of your dreams will be worth it all.

No one has to live a life of regret.

IT IS NEVER TOO LATE

Is it ever too late to realize your potential or to live out your dreams? No! Examples abound. Several months ago, I read an inspiring story about a couple who had recently sailed their homemade thirty-foot sailing vessel across the Atlantic Ocean. Crossing the ocean in a small boat isn't all that uncommon; what makes this story interesting is that the couple was a ninety-two-year-old woman and her sixty-eight-year-old son.

Their voyage was inspired by a dream the woman and her late husband nurtured for more than forty years. The husband had been building the boat, but he died before the vessel was completed. Since the dream was as much the woman's as it was her husband's, she asked a boat-building company to complete the project. However, the company went bankrupt before the boat was completed. Undeterred by this stroke of misfortune, the woman bought back the boat from the bankruptcy trustee, despite having paid in advance for the refurbishing that was never completed. Several years later, her son finished the vessel, and in doing so enabled his mother to live out her dream to sail across the Atlantic.

After several years of trying to persuade grocery stores to carry his new brand of popcorn called Red Bow, its creator was deeply discouraged. He turned to his spiritual tradition, Christianity, and read that "for waging war you need guidance, and for victory many advisors." Taking this verse to heart, he asked around for the name of a good marketing company. "A few days later I traveled to Chicago to seek guidance from my chosen advisors," he recalls. After describing his new popping corn to a Chicago marketing firm, they recommended the product be marketed as Orville Redenbacher's Gourmet Popping Corn. In addition, they recommended featuring his picture on the label! "I drove back to Valparaiso (Indiana) wryly observing we had paid $13,000 for someone to come up with the same name my mother had come up with when I was born," Redenbacher recalls thinking that day.

Today Orville Redenbacher's product is the best-selling popcorn in the world. However, his success began *after* he was reaching the age when most people choose to retire. Although a late bloomer, Orville Redenbacher is another example that it is never too late to start the adventure of pursuing a dream.

As writer George Eliot put it, "It's never too late to be what you might have been."

It is never too late to pursue a dream. Even rock-and-roll legend band Lynyrd Skynyrd has a song titled "Never Too Late"!

So don't listen to anyone who says you are too old to learn how to fly a plane, learn how to sail or scuba dive, start your own business, or go back to school. When your mind and heart are committed, dreams know no age boundaries.

The truth is, the phrase "I'm too old" is just one of the many excuses a person will be tempted to use when she is facing the scary life-changing choice to follow a dream.

You think you're too old? Colonel Harland Sanders founded Kentucky Fried Chicken at age sixty-five.

You think you don't have enough money? Sam and Helen Walton put up their house to finance the first Wal-Mart.

You don't have a college degree? Neither did Bill Gates, Steve Jobs, or Henry Ford when they started their businesses.

You've experienced rejection? Michael Jordan didn't make the basketball team in eighth grade.

You got fired from your last job? So were Lee Iacocca and Art Linkletter.

And the list could go on. These people didn't wait until everything was perfect before they pursued their dreams. Instead, they stepped through barriers by faith. And their steps of faith earned them the prize of seeing their dream realized.

The power of your attitude and faith has no age limit. It is your inner beliefs and attitudes, not your age, which will determine whether you will move forward or retreat, continue or quit, remain open to new opportunities or remain frozen in the past. History is filled with "old" people who accomplished great things:

✳ Moses was eighty years old when God called him to lead Israel to a new home.

✳ At age sixty-five, Winston Churchill became Britain's prime minister, where he then championed Britain's fight against Hitler's regime.

✳ Golda Meir became prime minister of Israel at seventy-one.

✳ Margaret Thatcher became Britain's first female prime minister at age fifty-three.

✳ Sadie and Bessie Delany wrote their first book when they were one hundred and five and one hundred and three, respectively. (The Delany sisters' *Book of Everyday Wisdom* became a best seller.)

✳ Samuel Hayakawa was elected to the United States Senate at age seventy.

Maybe you have a dream of owning your own business, or becoming an attorney, a real estate broker, a computer game programmer, earning a graduate degree, opening an interior design business, selling your artwork, or becoming a published writer. To be successful in any of these endeavors will take time, effort, and personal sacrifice. It will call for faith and perseverance on your part, but remember, "There are many choices, many paths one can take. Some paths will be easy. And their only reward is that they are easy." (Anonymous)

Don't use your age, or use anything else as an excuse for not stepping out toward your dreams. "Raise your sights and see possibilities," writes Norman Vincent Peale, "always see them, for they are always there."

LET'S GET STARTED!

We have spent these first two chapters discussing the nature of your dreams and the characteristics that make up those dreams. We discussed issues that prevent individuals from pursuing their dreams, and dismissed excuses people will be tempted to make as they consider taking a step of faith in a new direction.

In the following chapters, we will walk step by step through an engaging process that will help to further clarify your dreams and goals. You will also create a practical tool that will serve as a guide when you are finally ready to take those first courageous steps into your future. Hang on and enjoy the ride!

CHAPTER 3

What Do You Believe?

As you begin the journey toward your dreams, you must start by looking inside: looking inside your heart and mind to accurately assess the condition and health of your thinking, inner beliefs, and spirit. This is necessary because only after you've adequately prepared your *inner* life can you then confidently and effectively move *outward* in the direction of your courageous dreams.

Zig Ziglar writes, "The basic problem is that many people are afraid of their own dreams." This may seem odd, but for many people this statement is true. But why? Why would anyone be fearful of his own dreams and desires?

Dreams always lie outside your comfort zone. They exist outside your carefully planned daily routines, so chasing a dream will require that you step away from what is familiar and venture out into the unknown.

Coauthor of *The One-Minute Millionaire* Robert Allen writes, "Everything you want is outside your comfort zone." And if your dreams exist outside your comfort zone, then you're faced with a real problem.

The problem is that most of us *enjoy* life inside our comfort zones, for our comfort zones include many precious monuments that have taken years to build and manage—including our family circle, network of friends, current career path, favorite vacation spots, and our overall efficient and predictable weekly routine. So the reason many people are afraid of their own dreams is because they know if they are going to make an honest attempt to accomplish their dreams and goals, they'll need to do some hard work deconstructing what they spent years constructing!

For this reason, your comfort zone can easily turn into a prison of your own making. It can quickly become an environment that greatly limits your potential. On the other hand, your dreams continually call you out, serving as a constant reminder that you were never meant to live your entire life safely tucked away in your comfort zone. Your dreams remind you that whatever life you have constructed for yourself can, and should, be periodically revised and renovated.

Even the simple act of buying a car can conflict with a person's comfort zone. I recently pursued a smaller dream of mine, which was to purchase a new Jeep. I have owned Jeeps most of my life, and had my eye on a new make and model. But to make this dream a reality, I also had to deal with the frustration of changing the status quo of my daily routine and level of comfort.

In order to make this purchase a reality, I had to figure out a way to sell my current Jeep, spend time researching the new vehicle so I could negotiate a good price, visit various car dealerships (which I hate to do) and, since my current Jeep was completely paid for, come to peace with taking out a loan for the purchase. Over the course of a few months, I spent a good deal of time deconstructing my current vehicle situation, so I could reconstruct a preferred car to drive.

This simple example shows that in order to accomplish even this smallest of dreams, you need to come to peace with disrupting your current life, while also embracing the work and discomfort necessary to pursue a preferred future. And for this reason, pursuing your dreams will *always* take a certain amount of courage. Courage to step out into the unknown. Courage to step away from what is safe and onto a new path that will lead you in a new direction.

The following story reflects this type of inner fortitude:

It was a few weeks before Christmas 1917. The beautiful snowy landscapes of Europe were blackened by war. The trenches on one side held the Germans and on the other side the trenches were filled with Americans. It was World War I. The exchange of gunshots was intense. Separating them was a very narrow strip of no-man's-land. A young German soldier attempting to cross that no-man's-land had been shot and become entangled in the barbed wire. He cried out in anguish, and then in pain he continued to whimper.

Between the shells, all the Americans in that sector could hear him scream. When one American soldier could stand it no longer, he crawled out of the American trenches and on his stomach crawled out to that German soldier. When the Americans realized what he was doing they stopped firing, but the Germans continued. Then a German officer realized what the young American was doing and he ordered his men to cease firing. Now there was an eerie silence across the no-man's-land. On his stomach, the American made his way to that German soldier and disentangled him. He stood up with the German in his arms, walked straight to the German trenches and placed him in the waiting arms of his comrades. Having done so, he turned and started back to the American trenches.

Suddenly there was a hand on his shoulder that spun him around. There stood a German officer who had won the Iron Cross, the highest German honor for bravery. He jerked it from his own uniform and placed it on the American who then walked back to the American trenches. When he was safely in the trenches, they resumed the insanity of war.

—Author unknown
From *Stories for the Heart,* compiled by Alice Gray

The reason your journey toward your dreams starts with the "inside"—with establishing healthy patterns of thinking and belief—is because it's only when your inner life and convictions are strong that you'll have the courage and fortitude to step out toward a new dream.

The spiritual teacher Osho notes that courage is not the absence of fear, but embracing the presence of fear along with one's ability to face it. It's not a small thing, and will be an ongoing struggle. In *Courage: Explorations for Open Minds* he focuses not on great moments of courage, but on the *inner* courage that enables individuals to lead authentic and fulfilling lives on a day-to-day basis.

COURAGEOUS THOUGHTS

Teachers and philosophers throughout history have affirmed that people's thoughts and faith directly determined the level of success they eventually experience.

"As a man thinks in his heart, so is he." (King Solomon)

"According to your faith, so will it be done unto you." (Jesus)

"Life consists of what a man is thinking about all day." (Ralph Waldo Emerson)

"The actions of men are the best interpreters of their thoughts." (John Locke)

"You are today where your thoughts have brought you; you will be tomorrow where your thoughts take you." (James Allen)

"Be transformed by the renewing of your mind." (The Apostle Paul)

"Nurture great thoughts, for you will never go higher than your thoughts." (Benjamin Disraeli)

"People are just about as happy as they make up their minds to be." (Abraham Lincoln)

As you study individuals who courageously pursued a dream, you will find that they came from a variety of cultures, family backgrounds, economic privileges, and had various intellectual abilities.

But they all had one thing in common. They all understood the critical importance of actively controlling and edifying their thought-life as they journeyed toward their dreams. Those who courageously pursue their dreams understand that in order to change their lives, they must first change their thinking.

Your thoughts are important because they directly influence your behaviors and emotions, and your daily behaviors and emotions are what directly determine the level of success you'll eventually achieve. During the course of a day, the quality of my thinking impacts every attitude and behavior. Throughout the day, the quality of my thought-life (or lack thereof) directly impacts how I treat my wife, children, friends, and family cat.

I am one of those dads who gave in to getting a cat after years of pleading from my children. (Also, the fact that my mother gave the cat as a surprise Christmas gift to my children helped seal the deal.) Being that our cat is the family member for whom I care the least, it is often the first to know whether I have been thinking uplifting or negative thoughts during the day. But do not fear for my cat, for I am constantly working to control my thinking in positive and constructive ways. (In addition, my children do a very good job of protecting the cat—being sure to give me a smack on the rear end if I happen to give one to our little feline friend.)

In order to see your dreams realized, you must understand, and embrace, that it is the quality of your thinking that will directly determine how you behave each day, month, and year of your life. Every day, my thinking directly impacts the words I use; whether I choose to get out of bed in the morning and work out; if I exhibit patience with my wife; if I spend enough quality time with my children; if I believe God cares; if I stay on my diet; how I treat our family cat.

And the same is true for you as well. Every day of your life is directly impacted by the quality of the thoughts that flow through your mind. This is a foundational truth you have to understand if you are going to successfully pursue a dream.

IT ALL STARTS WITH COURAGEOUS FAITH

Before discussing how to control your thinking, I want to briefly mention the concept of faith. The pursuit of your dreams will always start with stepping out in courageous faith—faith in who you are, and faith in who you can eventually become. And the fulfillment of your dreams will be directly impacted by the size of your faith.

For example, if deep down you do not believe you can educate yourself for a better career, you will never take the steps necessary to go back to school. If you do not believe you will ever be able to save enough money for a family vacation to Europe, you won't do it. If you really do not believe you can lose twenty-five pounds, you will only give your diet a feeble attempt, and if you do not believe in miracles, I guarantee you will never see one: for as you will see, a fundamental law of life is that your faith, or lack thereof, will directly dictate what you actually experience.

Reaching your dreams and goals will necessitate having a strong understanding of the power of faith. I am not talking about a religious faith, though it definitely can be included. What I am talking about is having a faith where you fully embrace and believe that your dreams are attainable. It is being sure of what you hope for and certain of what you do not see, and it will only be this kind of faith that will enable you to finally step away from your comfort zone and out into the unknown toward your dreams and goals.

So how does one develop this kind of faith? If "the law of life is the law of belief," as Joseph Murphy writes, how do you strengthen your ability to believe? How does one become "sure of what we hope for and certain of what we do not see," as the Christian Bible says? Let's start by examining how your mind actually works.

The Science of Your Mind and the Power Behind Your Thinking

Politician and author Bruce Barton has written that "nothing splendid has ever been achieved except by those who dared to believe that something inside of them was superior to circumstance." A Muslim blog says, "Dare to be involved in your life. Dare to create the life you've dreamed about. Your dreams are waiting: all they need is you!"

We have all been given a significant and powerful gift, a free gift that puts any of our computer technology to shame. It's a gift that, if used properly, can impact your life in many awesome ways; if misused it can limit or even destroy you. This awesome gift is your *mind.*

Since your mind was given to you free of charge, many people take it for granted. In *The Strangest Secret,* mentor Earl Nightingale's classic talk, Nightingale teaches that all of the most priceless possessions we can ever own have *already* been given to us free of charge at birth. These priceless gifts include our mind, our body, our hopes, our dreams, our soul, our intelligence, and our capacity to give and experience love. But because these gifts are freely given to us, many individuals end up taking these priceless treasures for granted.

The reason is that we all have a tendency to place little value on things given to us for free while placing high value on objects we purchase with money. Yet the exact opposite is true. Everything that is of highest value in life has been given to us free of charge, while even our most cherished material possessions are of minimal importance and can be replaced at any time. Our homes, cars, savings accounts can all be replaced, but our mind, health, and the other priceless gifts mentioned above, if lost, can never be replaced. Sometimes we get so distracted by our material possessions that we forget how much more valuable are the gifts we *already* have.

After my wife, Martha, and I were married, I began to save money to purchase a new television. (I say "I" because Martha did not think we needed a new TV.) Back then, in the 1970s, most televisions had a nineteen-inch screen. But recently a new TV had been introduced with a twenty-seven-inch screen! And the more and more I thought about having a twenty-seven-inch screen, the more I found myself having to squint my eyes just to see what was on that old nineteen-inch screen. It did not take long before I was convinced a nineteen-inch screen was way too small. But with the twenty-seven-inch screen, I would be set for life, or so I thought.

In the process of saving for that new television, I found myself being more and more distracted by the whole purchase. I was watching for sales, considering brands, and researching various options. I found myself becoming frustrated with my new wife because she was gently reminding me of something I already knew deep down in my heart . . . that "possibly" we did not need a new television, and could "possibly" better use the money to pay down our student loans.

Well, we eventually bought the television. But I distinctly remember how I allowed that purchase to negatively affect what was more important: my relationship with my wife. For a time, I valued that purchase over open and honest communication with Martha. I placed a higher value on having a new twenty-seven-inch television than on having a healthy relationship.

(This is a lesson that I am still learning, by the way. In fact, as of this writing, do you know they have now come out with a flat seventy-two-inch screen! And I am telling my wife, that "all I want" is a fifty-inch screen. And then I'll be set for life. We'll see how it goes.)

Don't ever become so distracted by your material possessions that you ignore more valuable treasures, including relationships, your health, and especially your mind. Instead, be diligent in placing, protecting, and effectively using these free gifts that allows us to think, create, and live exciting and fulfilling lives. As mentioned, one of these free gifts is the mind. And since you've been given such a powerful and awesome gift, you should be a diligent student of how it works. You need to understand how your mind was created to function and how it can be effectively used to help you successfully pursue your dreams.

In *The Powermind System,* scientist and author Michael Kiefer provides a good model for understanding your mind and how to leverage its power in your life. Though your brain functions as a single unit, it consists of three primary "parts," with each part fulfilling a specific role. The three parts include the conscious; the subconscious; and the super-conscious.

The Conscious Mind

The *first* part is the conscious mind. The conscious mind is where your logical and rational thinking takes place. This is the area of your brain that chooses whether to buy a television with a fifty-inch screen or a seventy-two-inch screen, and is the part of your mind that remembers (or forgets) your spouse's birthday, and then chooses how to celebrate that special event. It is also active in choosing how many scoops of ice cream you will get, and what toppings will cover it. The conscious mind plays a major role in the moment-by-moment decisions you make during the course of each day.

The conscious mind has the capacity to assess a situation and then make a decision. For that reason, you're usually very aware of the choices being made by your conscious mind. For example, if you're female, you are probably very aware of what outfit you'll choose to wear to an event this evening. If you're male, you will be very aware of which sporting events you'll watch on your new fifty-inch television set over the weekend.

Your conscious mind will be very active in identifying your dreams and goals. Then, after they are defined, your conscious mind will also be used to carefully create a plan to accomplish those dreams and goals.

It is critical to understand that the conscious mind also has the ability to "program" your *sub*conscious mind. This means that when a goal or objective has been chosen, your conscious mind can also instruct, or command, the subconscious mind to help you carry it out. In this way the conscious mind "programs" your subconscious mind.

Once you have sifted through the data and made a choice (for example, where you stand on a certain political issue, say regarding the pro-life/pro-choice debate), then this conscious choice will be sent and programmed into your subconscious. Once in the subconscious, this new "value" will start to influence many of your future choices and behaviors, even in ways which you may not be fully aware.

The Subconscious Mind

The *second* part of the mind is the subconscious. The subconscious is where your instinctive, intuitive, wisdom, and values-based "reactions" live. Your subconscious forever stores your values, beliefs, and experiences that are later used to influence and guide the decisions made in the conscious part of your mind (though its influence is often unnoticed).

In addition, the subconscious mind operates many of the ongoing functions of your body—like your heartbeat, digestive system, growth and repair of your body, and so on. Your conscious mind doesn't pay much attention to these activities because they are all naturally controlled by the inner resource of the subconscious mind. The subconscious is also where your emotions, thinking patterns, and memory are seated.

One critical characteristic of the subconscious is that it serves as a "goal-seeking" machine. The subconscious will strive to attain any specific goal and command given to it by the conscious part of your mind. In this way, your subconscious mind is very "programmable," for once it has been assigned a goal, or task to complete, it will work day and night behind the scenes to help make that goal a reality.

I live in central Illinois, home to some of the richest soil in the United States. During the planting season each spring, farmers can be seen working late into the night planting seed in the fertile, black soil. And each fall, it is amazing how the rich Illinois soil produces a generous and bountiful crop.

Your subconscious is very much like the black soil in which these farmers plant their seeds each spring. As with soil, the subconscious readily accepts whatever seeds are planted into it, good or bad. Just as the rich soil in central Illinois will accept seeds of corn as readily as the seeds of poison ivy, so will the subconscious readily accept what is planted into it, whether good or bad; your subconscious mind doesn't have the power to reject what is sent to it by the conscious mind. It cannot determine whether the conscious thoughts you plant are good or bad, true or false. If your conscious mind allows, the subconscious mind will embrace destructive beliefs, thoughts, and goals just as readily as positive ones. And whatever is planted in your subconscious will produce fruit.

One of the laws governing creation that most, if not all, world religions share in common is the law of sowing and reaping. This law states that "whatever a person plants, so shall they reap," whether it be seeds in the soil or thoughts in the mind. A corollary then would say that whatever is planted in our subconscious mind *will* produce fruit.

This is why people experience what we call self-fulfilling prophecies, for seeds planted in their subconscious mind from thoughts such as: "I will never be rich," "I will never be happy in our marriage," "I have made too many mistakes to ever be successful or happy," or even "I am not smart enough to learn how to program the DVR" eventually bear fruit and become reality. Once these thoughts and beliefs are planted into the deep soil of your mind by your conscious thinking (and spoken words), then your subconscious mind will work to make them a reality.

Your subconscious mind will never argue with you; it will readily accept whatever your conscious mind decrees. If you say, "I can't afford it," your subconscious mind will work to make it true. If you tell yourself, "I am ugly," your subconscious will ensure this becomes a reality. If you think, "I will never be able to kick my bad habit," your subconscious mind will make sure you never will. So it's critical that you respect and understand this fundamental law of sowing and reaping, for, according to Joseph Murphy, PhD, "what you write on the inside, you will experience on the outside."

So what are you to do with this knowledge regarding how the subconscious mind is programmed and influenced? How do you make sure your subconscious is used in a positive way?

The answer is simple: you continually and intentionally feed your mind with seeds of affirming faith, belief, and positive goals.

You have to renew your mind by continually feeding it with affirming truths about yourself. Then you need to develop daily disciplines that will drive these truths deep into your subconscious mind. This is where the heroic war will be fought, because it's in the battlefield of your mind that the seeds of your courageous dreams will either be protected and nurtured or washed away by destructive thoughts of fear and doubt.

In my own pilgrimage toward my dreams, the biggest battle I have had to fight along the way has been the one against my own fears, lack of faith, and negative self-talk. For many years I've struggled with doubts and negative self-talk about my own abilities and competence. I struggle with thoughts like "I am not good enough to succeed," "This will never happen for me," and other forms of mental trash. But I also know that if I'm going to step out to pursue my dreams, I need to quit programming my subconscious with trash and replace it with seeds of truth, truth about myself and my abilities.

Individuals with low self-esteem will restrict their potential, for no one can ever outperform their own self-image, no matter what level of potential they have. Michael Kiefer writes that "people do not act according to their true potential, they act according to their self-image belief about their potential. They behave consistent with their self-image."

Always remember:

"Whether you think you can or think you can't—you are right." (Henry Ford)

"We become what we think about." (Earl Nightingale)

"A man is what he thinks about all day long." (Ralph Waldo Emerson)

"As a man thinks in his heart, so is he." (King Solomon)

What you expect to happen usually does, because your mind will naturally work to bring into reality *any* goal on which you vividly focus. This fundamental truth will have a significant impact on whether you ever successfully reach your goals and dreams in life.

The Super-Conscious Mind

The *third* part of the mind is the super-conscious. The super-conscious is the spiritual component of the mind that some people have defined as the human spirit or soul. The super-conscious may be hard to accept for those who have been conditioned to hold a narrow view of human nature, believing humans are just advanced animals without any spiritual dimension.

This is where, according to many spiritual traditions, dreams originate, both the ones you experience when asleep and the ones you envision as future goals.

The super-conscious is the part of your mind that can connect with the spiritual realm and others through means we don't yet fully understand. Research has shown that we only use about ten percent of our brains. My bet is that a significant part of the other ninety percent deals with the power and function of both our subconscious and super-conscious, or the part of our mind that can connect with God, the universe, or the supernatural. It's important to recognize that every major religion teaches that people have a spiritual dimension that directly impacts their thinking, beliefs, and self-image.

I don't know what you personally believe regarding the existence of a supreme being or the spiritual realm, but I know deep within my heart there is more to this life than simply paying our bills for eighty years and then passing the checkbook on to the next person after we are gone.

As you start to go deep inside yourself to clarify your dreams, you'll need to be in touch with the spiritual realm. For me, walking through the woods or sitting by the ocean in a beach chair are moments where I like to pray and connect with God, which is one way my religious tradition connects spirituality. There's nothing like the peacefulness of walking in a forest, or the majesty of hearing the breakers crash on the shoreline, to help usher me into the presence of something greater than myself. For whatever reason, these places help me connect with my Creator.

I personally believe God not only created me but wants to help me live a courageous life. And this is exciting, because I know I have a partner in this journey who wants to lead and sustain me when I reach junctures where I do not know where to go, or what to do next.

Your own spiritual tradition will guide you on how to use the super-conscious mind. The perspective from which I speak is Christian-centered, for it is the best way for me to explain how I do this.

Positive Faith, Belief & Thinking
(Keeping a positive frame of mind)

I remember being told as a child that I could be whatever I wanted in life. To be honest, even as a child, I never believed that statement. I just didn't believe I could be an astronaut, a coach in the NBA, or a race car driver. My mind kept coming up with excuses why I would never achieve these dreams. Even now, when I tell my children that they can be anything they want to be, I see the doubt in their eyes.

Though I agree the phrase "you can be whatever you want to be" is simplistic, I also believe it's fundamentally true. But we drastically limit the power of this truth by our lack of faith and self-doubt. Author of *Rich Dad, Poor Dad,* Robert Kiyosaki, writes, "We all have tremendous potential and gifts. Yet, the one thing that holds all of us back in some degree is self-doubt. . . . As a teacher, I recognized that it was excessive fear and self-doubt that were the greatest detractors of personal genius."

Before we move on, I'd like to focus on how to properly program your subconscious mind with powerful thoughts of faith and belief. The first choice leading to success is the decision to take full responsibility for your thinking. You have to capture your thoughts and make sure they're feeding your subconscious with truth instead of self-limiting lies. But since your mind is constantly thinking, thinking, thinking, how do you effectively control this inner dialogue? On which thoughts should you focus, and which ones should you limit? And how is this actually done?

The first step to controlling your inner dialogue is to simply take a few days to observe your "self-talk." What are you saying to yourself? Everyone has an inner voice that is constantly talking to him. Your self-talk is what you tell yourself when you first look at your reflection in the mirror every morning, and it continues to speak to you throughout the day until you fall asleep in your bed at night. It's your "observer" who sits in the corner, watching everything you do.

Right now, as I write on my laptop, my inner voice rambles on. It fills my mind with continuous thoughts—some of which are positive, some negative. For example, I just had a positive inner dialogue a few minutes ago that went something like this: "Man! You are really making some good progress on this book. The words just keep flowing onto the page. You're such a writing genius!" But the negative self-talk is right there too, saying, "You're just wasting your time. Who are you fooling? This book will never get published. Why don't you get a life?" And so this inner dialogue goes on and on. But I have learned that, though this voice will continue to speak into my mind, it can be controlled.

What are your thoughts saying to you? Your inner dialogue may include statements like: "You look wonderful today!"; "That was a nice thing you did for your friend"; "Good job!" But if left unchecked, negative comments can also fill your mind with mental trash like: "You look like crap today"; "You are out of control with your eating"; "Your dreams are a joke! Who are you kidding?"

These negative and critical statements are very dangerous because they're planting seeds into your subconscious mind that will produce the negative "self-fulfilling prophecies" we talked about earlier. Thus, to prevent those negative thoughts from severely limiting your potential, you have to make the ongoing *choice* to take those thoughts captive and replace them with empowering thoughts of faith and belief.

I'm a firm believer that a person can change the way she thinks—that a person can change her mental bias from a negative "the glass is half empty" mindset to a positive "the glass is always half full" perspective. I am confident of this, because it's a road I've had to travel myself.

In the past, I prided myself on being what I called a realist, on being a pragmatic thinker and decision-maker who chose not to believe in things I couldn't see, touch, or smell. I was a realist. A pragmatic intellectual!

The problem was, I was so much of a realist that I left little room for the wonders of life and the power of belief to invade my imagination and experience. While others around me were stepping out in faith toward their dreams, I was insulating myself from the risk and fears of pursuing my own dream by making a list of intellectual excuses why such-and-such a dream was unrealistic. While I would have never called myself a negative thinker, that's exactly what I was. My self-limiting thoughts and rational excuses created a comfort zone that protected me from the inherent risks of my own dreams and passions.

But deep down I was disappointed with myself; I knew my pragmatic thinking was just an excuse that kept me safely imprisoned in my comfort zone. It was only later in life, after some honest reflection and hard work, that I broke free of my overly pragmatic mindset and embraced the possibilities (and risks) of the courageous life. I started taking active steps toward my long-forgotten dreams and have never looked back.

So after you've surveyed your self-talk, what tools can you use to start steering your inner dialogue in positive and empowering ways? How can you shape the thoughts that guide and program your subconscious mind? For the remainder of this chapter, I'd like to focus on two practical issues. The first is how to control and shape your thinking, and the second is to discuss ways a person can program his subconscious mind in positive and constructive ways.

The Practice of Taking Thoughts Captive

I've heard people discredit positive thinking techniques by saying "it takes more than positive thinking to be successful." While I agree that reaching your dreams will take more than simple positive thinking (a specific plan is also needed), if you don't nurture a stream of thoughts in your mind that affirms "all things are possible for those who believe," I guarantee your dreams will forever remain dormant.

American psychologist and philosopher William James said, "The greatest discovery of my generation is that human beings can alter their lives by altering their attitudes of mind." Self-help author Jack Canfield points out that research has shown the average person talks to herself about fifty thousand times a day, and if left unchecked, eighty percent of that self-talk will be negative, having a destructive effect on her life. So how do you reshape your thinking?

Accept the Truth about the Power of Your Thoughts

The first step is to fully accept and believe that you'll never rise above the level of your thinking and faith. You need to fully embrace everything we've discussed so far about the power of your thoughts. If you do *not* deeply believe that you're a product of your thoughts, then you won't maintain the personal discipline required to take your thoughts captive and then remold them in positive ways.

If you're still not persuaded, I challenge you to read a few classics in the field of how our minds work. Even if you're already convinced, it would be wise to educate yourself on what others have to say about the power of our thoughts and mind. There are many good books, but the ones I initially recommend include:

- *The Power of Positive Thinking* (Norman Vincent Peale): With more than five million copies sold, it's an easy-to-read classic that's very effective in communicating its truths.

- A second book is *The Magic of Thinking Big* (David J. Schwartz): This book has sold over four million copies and helps one understand the importance of thinking outside one's comfort zone. It was after I read this book that I started to allow some of my dreams to resurface in my life.

- A third book is *The Greatest Miracle in the World* (Og Mandino): Another classic that explains how a healthy self-image is a key factor to living a successful life, while low self-esteem results in a "living death." Mandino helps the reader understand and improve his or her self-esteem.

 Another book is the classic *Think and Grow Rich* by Napoleon Hill. This title may turn off some prospective readers, but try to be flexible. Even if your dreams don't involve financial riches, this book outlines Andrew Carnegie's formula for success and achievement that you may find helpful.

 Finally, I recommend Earl Nightingale's classic talk, *The Strangest Secret*. Earl Nightingale is the grandfather of the self-improvement movement and this recording was one of the seeds from which the personal-development industry grew. I highly recommend you buy and listen to it while traveling in your car.

Memorize Truth

The second discipline to help transform your thinking is to memorize a few quotes regarding the influence of your thoughts. A few of the phrases I have memorized and pondered over the years include:

"All men are driven by faith or by fear." (Andy Andrews)

"According to your faith, so will it be done unto you." (Jesus)

"Therefore be transformed by the renewing of your mind." (The Apostle Paul)

"Take your thoughts captive." (The Apostle Paul)

"If you realized how powerful your thoughts are, you would never think a negative thought." (Mildred Norman)

"People are just about as happy as they make up their minds to be." (Abraham Lincoln)

"I tell you the truth, if you have faith . . . nothing will be impossible for you." (Jesus)

"A man is the product of his thoughts. What he thinks, he becomes. " (Gandhi)

This is a partial list of some simple quotes I've memorized to guide my thinking, and I encourage you to memorize your own set of quotes from books you read and from your own spiritual and cultural tradition. Find quotes that resonate in your heart. Then, as you commit them to memory, they'll be there, ready to resurface in your conscious thoughts to encourage you to believe in yourself and your ability to pursue your dreams.

Commit to Learn More

The third thing I did was to *continue* reading other books about the science of our minds and the power of faith. I find that I'm motivated by reading biographies that tell how certain individuals accomplished more than others thought possible. Read about those who persevered in their dreams, including the biographies of Abraham Lincoln, Dale Carnegie, Helen Keller, Lewis & Clark, Billy Graham, Mother Teresa, Winston Churchill, Pope John Paul II, Margaret Thatcher, and others who believed and persevered through many difficult times as they chased a dream.

Choose Who You Allow to Influence Your Life

Early on in this process, a friend told me that we're the product of two things: the materials/books we read, and the people with whom we spend time. Mark Twain was right when he wrote, "Keep away from people who belittle your ambitions. Small people always do that, but the really great, make you feel that you too can become great." The fourth action step to help reshape your thinking is to evaluate, and then make specific choices regarding, the people with whom you spend your time.

For example, I have a friend who is a half-empty type of person. Though he can be fun and creative, he has a way of making me feel like my ideas and dreams are flawed. He makes me feel judged and unsure of my ability, skills, and potential. Though at times I enjoy his company, I've also made the choice to limit my contact with him.

On the other hand, there's another person I know who is successful, energetic, positive, and who believes in himself and in those around him. Whenever I'm in his presence, he makes me feel I have what it takes to reach my potential and dreams. He's an individual with whom I need to deepen my relationship and with whom I want to spend more time. And I am doing just that.

There are people with whom you're currently spending time who, for whatever reason, drain you of your energy and belief in yourself. But then there are others who inspire you and "make you feel that you too can become great." The latter are the type of people with whom you need to proactively deepen your relationship. Though it will take initiative and time on your part, as these relationships grow, you will mutually gain from each other's energy, wisdom, and friendship.

They say that if you want to become a millionaire, you need to spend time with self-made millionaires. When you spend time with these people, you learn firsthand the mindset, beliefs, work ethic, and personal characteristics that have propelled them to success.

The same is true for those who want to pursue a dream. If you sincerely want to reach your dreams, then spend time with those who have already reached their own courageous dreams. Your time with them will expose you to the life lessons, courage, focus, beliefs, and thinking habits that have propelled these individuals to the top. Remember, you are greatly influenced by those with whom you spend your time, so choose wisely.

Record Your Thoughts

My fifth recommendation is to continually fight your negative self-talk with the help of a personal journal. What are the negative thoughts you struggle with the most? As already mentioned, I've had to overcome my own forms of "mental trash," so in my journal, off to one side of a page, I've made a list of the dominant lies I tend to think.

Then on the opposite side of the page, I've written a counterstatement that represents the truth.

For example, opposite my statement, "I am no good," I wrote the truth, "I am uniquely created and have the spirit of power, love, and self-discipline to help me become all I was created to be." Again, opposite the lie, "I do not have what it takes to succeed," I wrote the counter-truth, "I can do all things through God who gives me strength."

There is a powerful verse in the Christian Bible that is often used in popular culture as well: "You shall know the truth, and the truth will set you free." As you fight against defeating thoughts, one of the best weapons you can use is truth. Often you fill your mind with statements that are simply lies. Lies, which if believed, will hold your future in bondage. But the key you can use to free yourself from this bondage of lies is truth. For truth will always set you free.

Make a list of the mental trash you routinely tell yourself. Then get alone and think. Think about, and then write down, what the truth actually is. Truths like you are loved; you are capable of being and doing more; you are uniquely created; you can exert self-control; you have many blessings for which you can be thankful; you can go back to school; you can repair your self-image; you can heal a broken relationship. Be still, and let your heart speak. Write these truths in your journal and then review them daily. Through the use of conscious thought, emotion, and visualization, drill them deep into your subconscious mind every day. If you persist, in time these truths will take root and begin to set you free.

Analyze Your Fears

Sixth, make a list of your fears. Similar to the way you deal with lies, you can fight your fears with truth. But in addition to making a list of the corresponding truths to counter each fear you list in your journal, write one small step you can take that will help you overcome that fear.

For example, one of my fears was, "If I tried to write a book, I'd only be wasting my time, for many books never get published." My corresponding truth was, "Not only do I have the gift of writing (many have confirmed this skill of mine), if I do not write this book, on my deathbed, I will regret never having tried." Then, my action step was to carve out four hours a week to write, starting that week.

Philosopher Dr. George Addair wrote that "everything you want is on the other side of fear." This statement causes me to slow down and think about the consequences of allowing any fear to control decisions I make regarding my life, career, and goals. As President Franklin D. Roosevelt emphatically proclaimed during his first inaugural address, "The only thing we need to fear is fear itself!"

Apply Whatever Else You Learn Along the Way

Finally, as you read various books on the science of your mind and the power of your thinking, you'll be exposed to additional ideas and practical methods to help reshape your thoughts. Choose the methods that resonate with you and incorporate them into your daily life. I recently read *Attitude is Everything* by Keith Harrell, and in it he gives ideas about how to build and maintain a positive attitude. I've listed a few of his ideas below that may be helpful to you; I know they've been useful to me (I keep this list in my journal as a reminder):

❋ Affirm yourself verbally

❋ Know (discover) what motivates you

❋ Visualize success and the achievement of your goals

❋ Practice positive self-talk

❋ Use positive and enthusiastic greetings with people

❋ Show enthusiasm in everything

❋ Stay connected with God (spiritually centered)

❋ Use humor

❋ Keep physically fit

* Count your blessings every day

* Monitor what you see, read, and hear

* Set aside good time with your family

* Serve others

* Clearly know your passions and purpose

* Set goals (with deadlines)

How to Program Your Subconscious Mind

One function of your subconscious mind is to serve as an internal goal-seeking machine. Your subconscious mind will strive to attain any goal given to it by the conscious part of your mind, thus your subconscious mind is very "programmable." And once it's been assigned a goal or task to complete, it will work day and night behind the scenes to make that goal a reality in your life.

Have you ever had a specific problem that you just could not solve, only later to have the answer pop into your conscious mind at the oddest of times? That's your subconscious mind working to solve a problem while you carry on with the rest of your life. Later, after your subconscious mind spent hours sifting through all the data stored in your memory bank, it finally finds a solution and sends it forcibly back into your conscious mind. This ability of your subconscious mind is an awesome gift!

I remember racking my brain to figure out what to buy my wife for our twentieth wedding anniversary. (I knew what I wanted to buy for *me,* but I struggled to determine what she would really want.) Deep down I wanted to surprise her, but even after a lot of brainstorming, I just couldn't think of an idea that would excite her. I felt stuck.

Well, it was at that point my subconscious went to work, working behind the scene creating a solution for my goal. Then, about a week later, *bam:* the idea of taking her on a vacation in Mexico jumped into my mind. We have a good friend who works at a local travel agency, and she set us up with a very reasonably priced trip to an all-inclusive Mexican resort.

When that idea initially entered my mind, I was a little fearful about the cost. (Again, fears are always there, trying to derail dreams and creative ideas.) But my subconscious was already at work on that, too. A few days later, I had a new idea that helped pay for the trip. And we did have a fantastic twentieth anniversary.

Albert Einstein said, "The intellect has little to do with discovery . . . call it intuition or what you will, and the solution comes to you, and you don't know how or why." So how do you program your subconscious mind to work on your specific goals and dreams? As you read books about the science of the mind, you will get plenty of practical ideas on how to effectively program your subconscious.

The following is one method that is effective. In the book, *The Power of Your Subconscious Mind,* Joseph Murphy, PhD, provides the following guidelines:

To have your subconscious assist you with a specific problem, difficult decision, or when you fail to see a solution to a problem, do the following:

1. Begin to think constructively about the problem, decision, or situation. Do not allow any fears to set in; these fears will only confuse your thinking. Quiet your body and mind and try to solve the problem with your conscious mind. Focus your thoughts on the preferred solution, not on problems. Focus your attention.

2. As you allow your mind to think in a positive and relaxed way, remind yourself of any bit of knowledge you have that may help solve your situation. If no answer comes, hand it over to your subconscious mind prior to sleep, or another activity. Then move on with life.

3. Until your answer comes, at various intervals spend time thinking about, and visualizing, the *solution* in a relaxed way. Then after a few minutes, once again turn your situation over to your subconscious mind and move on with life.

4. Do not delay the answer by thinking the solution will take a long time to figure out. Believe you will get an answer—do not doubt.

5. Eventually the solution will come to you as a sure feeling, an inner awareness, or overpowering hunch where you know that you know. Follow this sure feeling with faith and confidence.

To have your subconscious help you effectively accomplish your dreams and goals, do the following:

Once you have clarified your dreams and goals, the process to program your subconscious mind will be very similar to what was just mentioned. Impress your dreams and goals into your mind by visualizing and thinking about the accomplishment of your dream. Every day, in a relaxed setting, visualize yourself having already accomplished your dream. Picture yourself making progress and having the courage to walk through your fears. Using very clear pictures in your mind, continue to do this at various relaxed settings throughout the day.

Your subconscious will then take your dream on as a goal and work to help you attain it. All of a sudden you will notice things you did not notice before, and you will have ideas that you never thought of before. And when you start to combine these ideas with active steps of faith, you will start to move toward your dreams. Yes, you will have to step through fears and doubts along the way, but you will be making progress. And step by step, through time, you will get there as your subconscious prompts you with a various list of ideas and plans. As these creative ideas come to mind, record them in your journal and then determine to take a step each day, however small, toward your dream. Remember that, according to artist and author Ron Scolastico, PhD, "If you would go every day to a very large tree and take five swings at it with a very sharp ax, eventually, no matter how large the tree, it would have to come down."

Take a swing at your dream every day and sooner or later your dream will fall into your life.

So far we have talked about pursuing the courageous life. Living a life where we clarify our dreams, and then courageously step out in faith to accomplish them. In the last chapter, I gave you a list of questions and suggestions to help start the process of clarifying your dreams. This chapter discussed the critical topic of our thinking, giving practical tools people can use to "take their thoughts captive," so their thinking will not sabotage their dreams.

In the next chapter we'll continue to clarify your dreams and then create a practical plan to help realize those dreams. Be strong! Be courageous! You'll never regret the work you are doing.

I end this chapter with a powerful quote from theologian Charles Swindoll:

"The longer I live, the more I realize the impact of attitude on life. Attitude, to me, is more important than facts. It is more important than the past, than education, than money, than circumstances, than failures, than successes, than what other people think or say or do. It is more important than appearance, giftedness, or skill. It will make or break a company . . . a church . . . a home. The remarkable thing is, we have a choice every day regarding the attitude we will embrace for that day. We cannot change our past . . . we cannot change the inevitable. The only thing we can do is play on the one string we have, and that is our attitude. I am convinced that life is ten percent what happens to me and ninety percent how I react to it. And so it is with you . . . we are in charge of our attitudes."

CHAPTER 4

Who Are You?

My wife recently read a story about an elderly woman who, in her farmhouse, has an old dictionary she keeps open on a book stand with a bookmark pointing to the word "change." The definition reads, "To exchange for something else."

The pilgrimage toward your dream will include coming to peace with the need for, and process of, change.

Change is where you're willing to exchange your old thoughts and behaviors for something better. Change is where you make the choice to trade your comfortable routines for a new way of living that will proactively lead to your dreams and goals being realized.

Thus far, we have learned that a person enters into the courageous life when she takes the time to clarify her dreams—and then makes the choice to step away from her comfort zone, and through her fears, toward those dreams.

Hopefully, with the use of your journal, you've started to create a list of possible dreams, and have clarified the specific fears and negative self-talk that, in the past, have prevented you from stepping out toward those dreams.

Socrates wrote that "the unexamined life is not worth living," and in this chapter we'll continue laying the foundation upon which your courageous life will be built. Remember, your dreams are already on the horizon and will become clearer as you prepare for their arrival by remaining faithful to this inner work. Abraham Lincoln wrote, "I will prepare, and someday my chance will come." Your dreams are coming. Stay diligent, as in this chapter we continue to prepare the soil of your heart and mind so that the seeds of your dreams can take proper root and grow strong.

DIGGING DEEP

I remember vacationing as a young child on a lake in northern Minnesota. Each summer we spent the week fishing, swimming, water skiing, netting crawdads, and listening to relatives discuss various topics that included life, family, and faith.

I specifically recall how, after we caught a fish at my grandfather's favorite fishing spot, I was in awe as I watched him take that fish, bonk it on the head with a hammer, cut it open, and proceed to clean out its guts with his bare hands. I truly admired his skill at cleaning and filleting a fish. My grandfather's expert use of a hammer, knife, and then his thumbs put to shame any dissecting project I ever did in middle school!

Those days up north were always an adventure. The cabin we stayed at each summer was situated on a bay, and my grandfather had told me how, many years ago, a logging barge had sunk right out in that bay. He also said that sometimes when swimming, he would find parts of that old sunken vessel on the bottom of the lake.

Having always been fascinated with ships, I grabbed some snorkeling gear and got to work "raising" that old barge. That summer, as I swam and walked around that bay, my feet would sink into the muck and mire, and every once in a while my foot would feel *something* . . . and I'd shout to my parents sitting on the dock, "Hey, I found something!" I would then dig down with my feet and hands and retrieve the sunken treasure.

I remember pulling up part of a toilet from the murky bottom (which of course could have come from anywhere), along with a kettle, a logging chain, and other maritime treasures. And for the next few summers, I always spent at least a few hours searching for sunken treasure out in that bay. Even today, when we visit that cabin, I look out over the waves and dream of the bounty still hidden under the water. I have told my two teenage boys about that old logging ship . . . but they'd rather ride the Jet Ski.

Each summer as I swam in and explored that bay, I found a treasure of some type. And as you take time in these chapters to study the condition of your *inner* life, you'll find your own priceless artifacts that will later assist you when you step out toward your dreams.

In the last chapter we discussed the priceless gift of our minds and how we can harness its power to pursue our goals. In this chapter we're going to do the critical work of digging up and clarifying our individual *values* and personal *strengths*.

The reason you need to have a clear understanding of your personal values is that your values play an important role in guiding your daily decisions and behaviors; and if you're going to successfully pursue the courageous life, you have to first clarify and understand the values that are forever shaping your actions and choices.

In addition, since all dreams are not created equal, an understanding of your values will help you prioritize which dreams ought to receive your focus, time, and energy.

Psychiatrist, neurologist, and Holocaust survivor Viktor Frankl wrote that "the truth is that as the struggle for survival has subsided, the question has emerged: survival for what? Even more people today have the means to live but no meaning to live for." Taking the time to clarify the specific values that influence your decisions and behaviors will help leverage your dreams in ways that give your life deeper meaning and significance.

In addition, in this chapter we'll clarify your strengths. As with values, the reason we need to be crystal clear regarding our personal strengths is that our natural abilities and talents provide the means to effectively accomplish our dreams. Yes, weaknesses need to be managed, but it will be our strengths that propel us, and then enable us to sustain the momentum needed to courageously advance toward a dream.

In their book *Soar with Your Strengths,* Donald O. Clifton and Paula Nelson share the example of how the Chinese have long been able to hold the Olympic gold medal in Ping-Pong. At the 1984 Olympics, when they again captured the gold medal, the coach of the Chinese team was urged by a reporter to "tell us about your team's daily training regimen."

"We practice eight hours a day perfecting our strengths."

"Could you be a little more specific?" asked the reporter.

"Here is our philosophy: If you develop your strengths to the maximum, the strengths become so great it overwhelms the weaknesses. Our winning player, you see, plays only with his forehand. Even though he cannot play backhand, and his competition knows he cannot play backhand, his forehand is so invincible that he cannot be beaten."

And so it will be with our dreams. Though we all need to properly manage our weaknesses, it will be as we continually develop and then utilize our strengths that we will make the most effective progress toward our dreams. Each one of us has specific abilities, which if understood and leveraged, can help us quickly advance in almost any area of our life, including the pursuit of a dream.

Dr. Howard Hendrix, a professor at Dallas Seminary, gives a test to his incoming seminary students. He hands each student a three-by-five card and says he is giving them a "simple test to see if they will succeed in ministry." He starts the test by asking his students to list on one side of the card their three biggest personal *weaknesses*—which the students usually complete quickly. Dr. Hendrix then asks his students to turn over the card and write their three greatest *strengths*. This time, many of the students just sit at their desks not knowing what to write. Dr. Hendrix then looks his students in the eye and teaches them a profound truth, saying "though you will need to manage your weaknesses throughout your career, if you do not have extreme clarity regarding your three biggest strengths, you will never make it in ministry."

The same is true for you and me. Many of us tend to know our weaknesses, yet struggle to identify what we are naturally good at and gifted by our Creator to do. Thus we wander through our life and careers never quite confident, never quite sure of who we are or what our life should be about. Just as with our personal values, our strengths serve as a window into our mind and heart, and taking the time to clarify them will make the pursuit of our courageous dreams much more straightforward and attainable.

Dreamers Are Pragmatically Self-Aware

This whole process of clarifying our personal values and strengths is a continuation of the inward journey we started in chapter two. The reason we are taking the time to grow in our self-awareness is because all too often we are strangers to ourselves. Leadership scholar Warren Bennis notes that self-knowledge is essential to living a successful life. He writes, "To become a leader, then, you must become yourself, become the maker of your own life." The process of knowing oneself is "the most difficult task any of us faces. But until you truly know yourself, strengths and weaknesses, know what you want to do and why you want to do it, you cannot succeed in any but the most superficial sense of the word."

Being self-aware will be vitally important because in order to live the courageous life, we will first need to know how to effectively lead *ourselves* through the obstacles and fears that will inevitably cross our path. So how does one become more "self-aware"? How does a person uncover the truth about who they are, and how they were created?

Prepare Yourself

First of all, prepare yourself for what you may find. As a teenager, I always wanted to be the life of the party, and so when with my friends

I worked hard to always be energetic, witty, and outgoing. During my teen years, and then into college, I tried to reflect an extroverted personality in various social settings. But in reality, at least concerning this aspect of my life, I was completely *not* self-aware. As I look back, I remember wanting to be an extrovert because I had observed that those who were more extroverted, or the life of the party, seemed to have more friends and be happier. I was wrong on both counts.

Later I began to realize that though I enjoyed the company of others, I valued time by myself—alone at a park, or spending time by myself reading a book in a corner booth at a local restaurant. I realized that God wired me as an introvert, a person who needed solitude and who was not going to be the life of every party. And though I admire those who have an extroverted personality (in fact I married one), I now recognize, and appreciate, that I was wired in a different way.

Self-awareness is one of the first steps of growth in many religions and spiritual traditions. For example, Sufis consider self-awareness an intrinsic part of the path to wisdom and union with the Beloved.

Many people do not know who they are, or how they are wired. Being self-aware is not easy, and comes only after you have taken the time to reflect and honestly examine questions like:

- ✻ Who are you?

- ✻ Are you an introvert or an extrovert?

- ✻ Are you reenergized by spending time with people, or by spending time alone?

- ✻ Are you a detail-driven and organized person, or are you organizationally challenged?

- ✻ Do you tend to make decisions with your mind or your heart?

- ✻ Do you have a natural tendency to view life as being half-full or half-empty? (If still "half empty," reread chapter three!)

- ✻ What experiences in your past have positively and negatively affected your ability to love and draw close to others?

✳ How do you tend to limit yourself?

✳ What are your fears?

✳ How would you characterize your self-talk?

✳ What have you found to be your all-encompassing life dreams and goals?

✳ Do you truly think the Chicago Cubs will ever win the World Series?

These reflective questions could go on and on. Questions like these take courage to ask, but it also takes self-discipline to actually slow down long enough to ponder the answers. Set aside a few pages in your personal journal to record your thoughts as you take the time to contemplate these and other reflective questions. Remember, this inner work will provide the fuel that will propel you forward in the courageous life.

Don't forget to bring your body into the equation. For Eastern religions, soul and body are intimately and intricately connected. Most Eastern journeys into self-awareness involve meditation, yoga, fasting, and other body-soul combinations to help one uncover their heart, passions, and dreams. No matter what your spiritual tradition, exploring these disciplines will be helpful. Ask yourself the questions listed above and sit with your thoughts for a while. Answers may not come quickly, but they will come.

Personality Profiles

Second, there are various personality profiles that give good insight into how a person is wired, and many of them can be taken free over the Internet. For example, the Myers-Briggs test has a strong reputation for providing accurate feedback regarding one's personality and style, and the Strength Finders test, created by Gallup Research, is highly regarded for helping pinpoint an individual's top five strengths.

Other validated personality tests include the DISC and Big Five profiles.

The key to reaping the benefits of these assessments is they must be reviewed and studied: you have to use them! Many people take time filling out and initially reviewing an assessment, then file them away, quickly forgetting the information the profile provided. This is like looking at yourself in a mirror and then forgetting what you looked like after walking away. The mirror provided useful information about your appearance, but the feedback was ignored and quickly forgotten. This is a huge mistake.

When you take any type of personality profile, spend the following two weeks reviewing the results for a few minutes each day. Let the data provided in the assessment sink deep into your subconscious where your mind can work the results over and over until, at some point, the subconscious feeds your conscious thoughts with specific insights and action steps. In addition, a couple times each year, review your profiles again in a quiet setting. As the insights from these reports are allowed to drift in and out of your mind on a regular basis, your mind will prompt you with specific ways to effectively leverage this information for your own good and growth.

Seek Friendly Feedback

Third, seek feedback regarding your personality from those who know you very well—and even from those who do not. I have a love-hate relationship with the whole concept of feedback. I want to believe I am already perfect. Not only that, I also want *others* to believe I am already perfect. I want to believe that, besides possibly changing the habit of cracking my knuckles, not much correction is needed in my attitude and behavior.

But as you might suspect, my wife, children, friends, and even our family cat know very well I still have a long way to go. And in order to more fully understand where I still need to improve, I require their honest feedback (except from the cat that is). Leadership expert Ken

Blanchard had it right when he wrote that "feedback is the breakfast of champions."

If you want to achieve your courageous dreams, you will have to learn how to ask honest and courageous questions. I challenge you to ask two people every month to provide feedback regarding your personality, strengths, weaknesses, and other areas of conduct. What do they enjoy the most about your personality? What do they enjoy the least? Do you have any personality quirks? When do they feel the most relaxed around you? How do they see you limiting yourself? Taking the initiative to regularly seek out constructive feedback from people you respect will provide extremely valuable information for your own personal growth.

We are all blind to ourselves in various ways. We just do not see ourselves for who we really are. One reason other people come into our lives is so they can help us understand ourselves more accurately and provide useful insights to how we can more effectively grow and reach our potential. As the African proverb says, "Alone, I have seen many marvelous things, none of which were true." The fact is, we do not see reality without the help of others.

Still, remember that the feedback we receive is just that . . . feedback. It's just information that we can use, or not use, as we consider how to better grow and reach our potential.

Study Yourself

Finally, take time to observe yourself in *action*. Be a student of yourself by paying attention to the *results* your life is creating. Are you overweight? Are you happy? Do you have cherished friendships? Do you feel close to God? What are your healthy habits? What are your unhealthy habits? What mixture of results is your life currently producing, and why? Be honest as you step back and assess which areas of your life are going well, and where you can make improvements.

For example, I have learned from observing myself in my marriage that I "feel" loved when my wife does two things. First, I feel loved by

Martha when she proactively sets aside quality time to be with me on a consistent basis and second, I appreciate intentional acts of service. It was only after this realization that I was then able to discuss these with my wife, and her findings with me, which has helped us to communicate our love for each other in more effective ways.

The reason you want to continually grow in your self-knowledge is because the process of pursuing your courageous dreams is, in reality, a process in which you are becoming more and more who you were originally created to be. And you can never *become* that being until you first *know* who that being is.

YOUR DREAMS RISE FROM YOUR VALUES AND STRENGTHS

Before we walk through a few practical methods on how to clarify your specific values and strengths, let's talk a little more about *why* your values and strengths will play such a critical role in helping you pursue your dreams and goals.

Like a ship sailing across the open sea, your *values* represent the rudder that will guide you through the dangerous waterways and reefs that inevitably cross your path as you sail toward your dreams. And in similar fashion, your *strengths* will serve as the majestic sails, enabling you to most effectively and powerfully reach your destination. Having clarity regarding your personal values and unique strengths enables you to not only reach your courageous goals, but to reach them effectively.

I am deeply motivated to live a life with no regrets. On my deathbed I want to be able to say to myself, and to those around me, that during my time here on earth I made a faithful and all-out effort to reach my full potential. I *also* want to be able to say that I reached this potential in ways that did not compromise my personal values or integrity.

For example, as mentioned before, one dream of mine has been to write this book. Whether or not this book ever gets published is not relevant to me right now—I just know in my spirit this is a project that needs to be completed. But even as I confidently pursue this dream, I understand this dream should not be pursued in a way that compromises my core values, which are (in order of priority):

- Faith (intimacy with God)
- Family (intimacy with my family)
- Authentic relationships with others
- Reaching my full potential—being purpose-driven
- Life balance
- Freedom
- Self-discipline/self-control
- Being relevant

I hasten to add that these may not reflect your core values, nor should they. I am a product of my time, my background, my race, my spiritual faith, and a plethora of other influences, as are you. So bear that in mind as you read my list, and then create your own. For example, my personal value "intimacy with God" reflects my Christian faith; if you do not share that belief, don't let it stop you. Take time to discover and write down the core values that you want *your* life to reflect.

So while writing this book aligns with my value of "reaching my full potential," I am careful not to compromise other core values in the process, especially those I hold as a higher priority. In fact, just a few minutes ago, I got a call from my wife asking if I would like to meet her and our son for lunch. When my wife called, I was on a roll in my writing. Words were flowing, my fingers were typing on my laptop as fast as they could go, and I feared losing some critical thoughts if I left for lunch. But at the same time, my conscious mind was reminding me of my second-highest value, which is to enjoy intimate relationships with my family, and I knew this would be a perfect opportunity to do just that. So I made the *choice* to pack up my laptop and head off to the restaurant. The window of years I have with my son are limited and quickly closing, and I will have many years to write books after he has left for college.

Be sure of this, taking the time to become crystal clear regarding your values (and strengths) will ensure that through life, and eventually on your deathbed, you will know you accomplished your courageous dreams *with* those you loved, not at the expense of those you loved. In fact, clarifying your values and strengths will provide the following *four* navigational guides that will enable you to safely sail the mighty waters toward your courageous dreams:

First, clarity regarding your personal values and strengths will help *define* your dreams and goals. I would argue that until you've completed the process of discerning, in order of priority, your life values— and have clarified your unique and God-given strengths—you will never be able to precisely determine your dreams and goals in life.

As a young adult, I only had a minimal understanding of my values and strengths. Throughout high school, teachers told me that since I was good at math and science I should pursue a degree in engineering, which I did. Four years later, after graduating, I started my career as an engineer for a local utility company. Although I enjoyed this first job, in my spirit I still felt discontented. So I soon went back to school to complete a graduate degree, thinking more education might ignite the passion I knew was lacking.

During those years I was also volunteering for a youth ministry that helped students navigate their "turbulent teenage" years, while guiding them in their faith. I enjoyed the work so much that I eventually made the difficult choice to leave my engineering job to pursue ministry as a full-time career. And though I enjoyed my years in the engineering world, I have never regretted my choice to leave, for I knew that working with students was a better fit to my personal values. Then again, sixteen years later, my values played a major role as I went through the difficult process of deciding to leave my career in ministry to pursue a new dream to help individuals and organizations clarify, and then reach, their potential.

In a similar fashion, clarifying my personal strengths has also helped me to accurately define my dreams. My strengths, as I have discerned them, are:

- ❋ Wisdom & discernment

- ❋ Systems thinking

- ❋ Focus (I focus well on tasks)

- ❋ Intentional relater (good at intentional relationships)

- ❋ Facilitating growth & learning

- ❋ Creative writing & teaching

- ❋ Listening

Every career choice I have made has brought me closer to a profession that more effectively uses my personal strengths and abilities. As I have discovered and embraced my natural abilities, I have been able to wisely move into new careers that allow me to more effectively use these natural gifts and strengths.

For example, when I was in high school, I worked construction jobs each summer where I would sweat like crazy pouring concrete basements, framing houses, and installing insulation. While I enjoyed being outside and working with friends, deep down, I knew the construction industry was not my life calling.

Later, while working as an engineer, I did have the opportunity to use more of my natural strengths, but as I mentioned, engineering did not align close enough with my core values, thus prompting my decision to enter youth ministry. Sixteen years later, consideration of my strengths came to the forefront again as I made the decision to leave ministry and enter a career as an organizational consultant.

Second, clarity regarding values and strengths provides the *fortitude* and *determination* needed to pursue a dream. Winston Churchill once quipped, "The nose of a bulldog has been slanted back so he can breathe without letting go." Being clear regarding our values and strengths does the same for us. Just as the nose of a bulldog allows it to continue pulling and tearing at what it wants, so our values and strengths equip us to keep fighting for our courageous dreams.

There are many people who are aware of their weaknesses, but struggle to define what they are naturally good and gifted to do. And thus they wander through life, de-energized in their careers and never quite sure of who they are, and what their life should be about. As a result they find it hard to persevere through the difficulties that always occur when anyone steps out toward a dream.

Viktor Frankl, survivor of three grim years at Auschwitz and other Nazi prisons, recorded his observations of life in Hitler's camps in *Man's Search for Meaning.* He wrote, "We who lived in concentration camps can remember the men who walked through the huts comforting others, giving away their last piece of bread. They may have been few in number, but they offer sufficient proof that everything can be taken from a man but one thing: the last of human freedoms—to choose one's attitude in any given set of circumstances, to choose one's own way."

When Viktor Frankl lived those years in various camps, what strength and core values gave him the fortitude to withstand the horrors he experienced? When you read his essays, you will find that one of Frankl's core values (and strengths) was his strong belief in a person's "freedom to choose one's attitude" in any circumstance. And it was this firmly held conviction that gave him the fortitude to endure everything that happened to him there.

Your values and strengths provide staying power. They provide the stern fortitude and confidence to continue pursuing a dream, even when circumstances seem to be working against you. Clarity regarding your values and strengths can stir within you the "fight of the bulldog," fueling your determination to hold on and fight for the dreams you feel compelled to pursue.

Abraham Lincoln had extreme clarity regarding the values that directed his life and presidency. Lincoln constantly shared and emphasized two fundamental beliefs that guided his stance on various issues: the pursuit of liberty and equality. For Lincoln, the Civil War was not just a conflict in arms, but rather a "people's contest." "On the side of the Union," he said, was "a struggle for maintaining in the world that form and substance of government whose leading object is to elevate the condition of men . . . to afford all an unfettered start, and a fair chance, in the race of life."

Any student of Lincoln will learn that the difficult decisions he made while president were intimately directed by his guiding values, while his personal strengths (two of which were patience and perseverance) were effectively leveraged to carry out those courageous and historic decisions.

Third, clarifying your values and strengths helps keep your *motives* pure. Many times I am a selfish and prideful person. I have been known to hide the Girl Scout cookies from my kids so I can later have them all to myself; I too often insist on controlling the remote when our family is watching television; and when no one is looking, I often break my own rule of drinking juice directly out of its refrigerator container. The Catholic monk Thomas à Kempis wrote, "Be not angry that you can not make others as you wish them to be, since you cannot make yourself as you wish to be."

Although your motives are rarely completely pure, you do need to take full responsibility for them because, as reflected in the poem on the following page, your selfishness can quickly distract you from what is truly important in life.

This is a mother's poem of regret, a heartfelt reflection back on a time when her selfish desires distracted her from what truly mattered. The same regrets are reflected in Harry Chapin's song "Cat's in the Cradle." And I know from experience that my ego, selfishness, and pride can often get in the way and also distract me from what is most important.

Being clear about your values helps you choose wisely. When my wife invited me to lunch, my life values flashed into my mind, helping

To My Grown-Up Son
(Author Unknown)

My hands were busy throughout the day;
I didn't have much time to play
The little games you asked me to—
I didn't have much time for you.
I'd wash your clothes, I'd sew and cook;
But when you'd bring your picture book
And ask me please to share your fun,
I'd say: "A little later, son."

I'd tuck you in all safe at night,
And hear your prayers; turn out the light,
Then tip-toe softly to the door . . .
I wish I'd stayed a minute more.

For life is short, the years rush past . . .
A little boy grown up so fast,
No longer is he at your side,
His precious secrets to confide.
The picture books are put away;
There are no longer games to play.
No good-night kiss, no prayers to hear—
That all belongs to yesteryear.

My hands, once busy, now are still.
The days are long and hard to fill.
I wish I could go back and do
The little things you asked me to.

me make the wisest choice. A choice that now, much later in the afternoon, I do not regret. I had a very nice lunch with Martha and our son, while also making good progress in my writing.

In a similar fashion, being clear regarding your *strengths* helps to keep your motives and priorities pure. I was recently asked if I wanted to play bass guitar in a local band. Some day I sincerely hope that playing the bass guitar will be a developed skill of mine, but since I have been playing for only a few years, I have a ways to go. Somehow, the person heard I was "a really good bass player" (which I neglected to deny) and wondered if I wanted to be in his band. A surge of energy flashed through my body as I heard this request. You see, I have another dream . . . it is the desire to play bass guitar for Bruce Springsteen, U2, or Shania Twain. I figure that if one of their bass players meets an early demise, I could step right in and help.

But just like the time my wife called to ask me to join her and our son for lunch, when I was asked to play in this local band, my list of strengths flashed into my mind—and as you see listed above, playing bass guitar is not on it. And though playing bass is a hobby of mine, it is not (yet) a strength. This realization helped hold my ego in check, and prevented me from becoming distracted by some secondary fantasy.

You'll be continually confronted in life with a variety of opportunities and choices, and many of these opportunities will inevitably tug at your selfish ambitions and egos. But it you've taken the time to honestly clarify your guiding values and strengths, you'll have the baseline knowledge needed to make wise choices that keep us centered and focused on the right things.

Finally, when you clarify your values and strengths, your *subconscious* mind then has valuable information to use as it guides you in the courageous life. As I mentioned in chapter three, your subconscious is where your instinctive, intuitive, and values-based reactions spring from. Your subconscious forever stores your values, beliefs, and experiences, which are later used to influence and guide the decisions made by your *conscious* mind. The subconscious is programmed by whatever thoughts are sent to it, and will work diligently to produce fruit in accordance with what is planted in its "soil."

When you have clarity regarding your strengths and values, your subconscious will help you see opportunities that align closely with those strengths and values. Now that I am clear as to what my personal strengths and values are, my subconscious mind can continually look for opportunities to express them—and also help prevent me from being distracted by situations that do not align with who I am, or how I am gifted.

A business opportunity recently crossed my path that on the surface seemed very enticing because, quite frankly, I could make a lot of money if it succeeded. To be honest, though making money is not one my top five values, it's something I enjoy. When presented with this opportunity, my subconscious was sending strong and clear warnings into my conscious mind, which I tried to ignore. My subconscious was cautioning me in two ways—one, that the competencies needed to pursue this opportunity did not align with my personal strengths, and two, since this opportunity would require considerable time and travel for two or more years, a decision to move ahead would neglect my highly held values of family and life balance. Though I tried to suppress these guiding thoughts from my subconscious, it remained relentless in its dialogue with me, and as a result, I eventually passed on this opportunity.

When you go through the process of clarifying your strengths and values, and allow them to be planted into your subconscious, your mind will work diligently to find opportunities that will allow you to express these strengths and values in the most effective ways, yet without compromise.

In summary, as you pursue the courageous life, your values and strengths will be critically important in providing both guidance and fortitude as you step away from your comfort zone and on toward your courageous dreams.

You skip this inner work at your own peril. We have all known individuals who end up living lives of regret because they have, for whatever reason, neglected this inner work during their tenure on earth.

How to Clarify Your Personal Values and Strengths

As you continue to use your personal journal to clarify your dreams (chapter two), and your self-dialogue and fears (chapter three), let's review a few practical methods to clarify values and strengths. I encourage you to get away to a quiet place where you can spend a few hours thinking and working through these simple exercises:

Clarify Your Values

The purpose of this exercise is to help clarify the specific values that deeply influence your life. The most compelling source of purpose and energy is derived from intimately connecting your dreams to your deeply held values, for they will define an enduring code of conduct, or the rules of engagement, which will guide you on your journey. One method to explore the values that are most compelling for you is to set aside some uninterrupted time to reflect on these questions with the help of your journal:

- Imagine the end of your life. What are three of the most important lessons you have learned? Why are they so critical?

- Think of someone whom you deeply respect. Describe the three qualities in this person you most admire. (Ask this question about others you highly respect too.)

- What circumstances or settings bring out the best in you?

- Who are the people, and what are the issues, for which you are willing to die? Why?

- What values do you admire in others? What values do you want your children to personally embrace and live out in their lives?

- What one-sentence inscription would you like to see on your tombstone that would capture who you really were in this life? What values are reflected in this statement?

- What do you do really well? (This can be anything: hobby, work, craft, sport, etc.) What "feels right" about doing it? Why does this activity energize you?

- Recall a story (fiction or nonfiction) that inspired or impressed you in some way. How did you feel when you first heard the story? What values are represented in this story that resonate with you?

- Imagine you have been asked to write down the "secret of life" that you have learned over the years to pass on to future generations. Using the clearest and most descriptive language possible, what underlying values are included in your "secret of life"?

- Describe a success in your recent past that came as the culmination of hard work and dedication; something that you kept working on until it was right. What personal values were reflected in this project?

The Mountain Range Exercise

A second method to clarify your values is described in Alex Pattakos's book, *Prisoners of Our Thoughts.* This book provides a method adapted from Viktor Frankl in which you start by looking over your life as you'd look out over a mountain range.

Which individuals would you place on the peaks before you? In other words, who are the people who have influenced your career and life? These people may include authors, teachers, employers, leaders, or people in your life who have mentored and loved you. You can use colored markers to sketch out your mountain range and write on the peaks the names of these special individuals.

Now, along the mountaintops, write down the *recurring* values that were evident in the lives of these people. Explore the key values. Which are the most meaningful to you? Which of these values have you been the most committed to in your life and career?

The methods described above will help bring to the surface the values that will define your "rules of engagement" as you journey toward your courageous dreams. (A sample list of values is provided below). The objective is to determine which five to seven values are most motivating to you personally. Your initial list will merely be a first draft, for as you continue to reflect on your values, and become more self-aware, you will make revisions to words and phrases.

Once you have your first draft, review this list a few times each week and reflect on these values to determine if any revision or edits need to be made. Show your list to your spouse, or close friend, and get their feedback as well.

In chapter six I'll provide an easy format for listing your values, strengths, and dreams, but for now just keep a draft of your values in your personal journal.

First Draft of My Top Five to Seven Values:

1. _____

_____

2. _____

_____

3. _____

_____

4. _____

_____

5. _____

_____

6. _____

_____

7. _____

_____

A Sample List of Personal Values:

Accountability	Empathy	Honesty	Relationships
Assertiveness	Empowerment	Humor	Respect
Authenticity	Excellence	Integrity	Responsibility
Autonomy	Fairness	Kindness	Security
Balance	Faith	Knowledge	Self-Control
Beauty	Family	Learning	Service
Building	Flexibility	Love	Simplicity
Commitment	Freedom	Loyalty	Social Responsibility
Communication	Friendship	Mastery	Stability
Compassion	Fun	Openness	Structure
Competence	Generosity	Patience	Success
Courage	Growth	Patriotism	Teamwork
Creativity	Happiness	Perseverance	Trust
Discipline	Health	Recognition	Vision

Clarify Your Personal Strengths

The following exercises will help clarify your unique strengths. As discussed, to excel in life you will need to understand and leverage your special talents, skills, and abilities. You will need to become an expert at discovering, describing, applying, and refining the strengths that will drive your success. Our misfortune in life is not that we do not have enough strengths, but that we fail to use the ones we already have. Look inside yourself, identify your strongest abilities, and reinforce them with practice and learning. When you do, you will be more productive, fulfilled, and successful.

For an activity to be a personal strength, you must be able to do it consistently at a high level. As detailed in the book *Now, Discover Your Strengths,* by Marcus Buckingham and Donald O. Clifton, when discerning your personal strengths, be careful to consider three issues:

- **Your Talents**—Recurring patterns of thought, feeling, or behaviors that come naturally and seem to help you succeed at various tasks.

- **Your Knowledge**—Consists of the facts and lessons you have learned, and seem to understand well.

- **Your Skills**—Activities *you are highly competent in and enjoy doing.*

Any combination of *talents, knowledge,* and *skills* can create a personal strength.

To explore more deeply your unique set of strengths, set aside uninterrupted time and reflect on the following questions:

- Reflect on your talents, knowledge base, and skills—what would you say are your five to seven primary personal and professional strengths?

- What do you do best? What activities come naturally for you and which you can do consistently at a high level?

- What professional/job activities do you enjoy, do well, and find personally fulfilling?

- What activities do you, or have you, learned quickly and seem to accomplish with less effort, when compared with others?

- What do you naturally do well, and could be done with excellence after focused training?

- Meet with four others whom you respect, and who know you well. Ask them for specific feedback regarding what they believe to be your personal and professional strengths.

(A sample list of strengths is provided later.)

Now, Discover Your Strengths

The authors of the book just mentioned (*Now, Discover Your Strengths*) define a "strength" as being a combination of your personal talents, skills, and knowledge, which you consistently and productively apply to achieve superior results. They point out that "unfortunately, most of us have little sense of our talents and strengths. Instead, guided by our parents, our teachers, our managers, and psychology's fascination with pathology, we become experts in our weaknesses and spend our lives trying to repair these flaws, while our strengths lie dormant and neglected."

The Strengths profile provided in their book is filled out via the Internet and gives a very detailed survey of your top five strengths. Individuals from all around the world have taken this profile and have found it very helpful. I recommend you take the results and lay them alongside the list of strengths you have already compiled using the questions provided above. I also recommend running your top five strengths past a few friends who know you well for their insight and feedback. I have used this profile with many clients and have always been pleased with its helpful insights.

Again, in chapter six, I'll provide an easy format for listing your values, strengths, and dreams, but for now keep a list of your strengths in your personal journal.

First Draft of My Top Five to Seven Strengths:

1. _____

_____

2. _____

_____

3. _____

_____

4. _____

_____

5. _____

_____

6. _____

_____

7. _____

_____

Sample List of Strengths

Adaptable	Delegation	Fast Learner	Organizer
Analytical	Developer	Focus	Relational
Athletic	Discernment	Good Listener	Responsible
Casting a Vision	Disciplined	Integrity	Self-Starter
Coaching	Empathetic	Knowledge	Strategic Thinker
Communication	Encourager	Leader	Strong Beliefs
Competitor	Entrepreneur	Loyalty	Teaching
Confident	Ethical/Values Driven	Manager	Technical Knowledge
Connector	Facilitator	Maximizer	Wisdom
Coordinator	Fairness		

SO . . . WHICH DREAM?

The French aphorist Abbe' D'Allanival wrote, "The more alternatives, the more difficult the choice." Before we move on, I'd like to mention one additional critical role your values and strengths will play as you pursue the courageous life. As you have started your list of possible dreams, you may be wondering how does one pick which dream, or dreams, to pursue? This is the critical choice that will call for wisdom and discernment.

Years ago, when I first started to ponder what my dreams might be, included on my list was to write a book, start my own consulting firm, create a Web-based leadership resource business, move to the Caribbean, and so on. Now, the various dreams on my list may all one day be realized, but I needed to choose which *one* dream I would focus on first. Which dream I would step out to heroically pursue, and which dreams I would put on hold.

This is where being self-aware regarding my personal strengths and values were invaluable. The dream I initially chose to pursue was to start my own consulting business, for after much reflection and prayer I knew this dream aligned most closely with my personal values and abilities.

When you are ready to decide which dream to pursue, simply choose the dream that aligns most closely with your personal values and incorporates most of your strengths.

Talk-show host Oprah Winfrey has written, "I've come to believe that each of us has a personal calling that's as unique as a fingerprint— and that the best way to succeed is to discover what you love and then find a way to offer it to others in the form of service, working hard, and also allowing the energy of the universe to lead you."

Your values and strengths are part of your unique "fingerprint" that will help effectively lead you down the path toward your dreams. Respect them, and they'll pay huge dividends!

NEXT...

So far in this book, we've discussed various issues regarding the nature of your dreams and how your thinking, values, and strengths will play a critical role as you take steps to realize those dreams. With the help of your journal, you've taken the time to start formulating your dreams, while also clarifying your personal values and strengths, which will be wisely leveraged to accomplish those dreams.

Next, we are going to discuss one more "inward" issue before moving out in the direction of your courageous dreams.

CHAPTER 5

Your Mission in Life

In his song "Ready to Take a Chance Again" Barry Manilow describes the dissatisfaction a person will eventually start to feel if he chooses to remain in his comfort zone. And when these feelings of discontent and dissatisfaction surface, many individuals will try to suppress them by convincing themselves that their nice and comfortable life is indeed satisfying. As Manilow's lyrics note, these individuals may succeed in convincing themselves for a while—but eventually someone, or something, will come along and confront them with the truth.

Your heroic dreams *always* lie outside your comfortable and "very nice" (as Manilow describes it) life. Your dreams always lie out there . . . somewhere. And though the path leading to your dreams will not always be clearly marked, and barriers must be overcome along the way, a choice will always be required.

That choice is whether or not we are willing to "take a chance" and join the small contingent of others who have already stepped away from their "nice" lives to courageously journey toward their dreams. Are *you* ready to step out and take that chance as well?

THERE MUST BE MORE

Do you ever wonder if there is more? Do you ever sense there must be more to life than what you are currently experiencing? Understand that this feeling of unrest is a priceless gift intended to prevent you from living life within the walls of your comfort zone.

In his book *Maximum Achievement,* best-selling author and professional development speaker Brian Tracy writes, "Fully 80 percent of people working today would rather be doing something else, and 84 percent of them, by their own admission, feel that they are working below, or even far below, their potential. Only 5 percent feel they are producing at their full capacity in their jobs. . . . America is a free society. All choices are open to the individual. People can do anything, be anything, go anywhere, change any part of their lives for the better, whenever they want. . . . Why is it that so few people are living up to their potential?"

Again, this feeling of unrest felt by 84 percent of people is a gift. You see, I believe you were created with an internally wired Potential Indicator (PI), which constantly sends signals into your conscious mind indicating whether or not your life is on track to reach your potential.

When your life is on a path leading to the realization of your true potential, this PI infuses your mind and heart with energy, creativity, wisdom, and other supportive assistance to help maintain the steps you're currently taking toward that potential. When you aren't living up to your potential, your PI will send a stream of subtle feelings of unrest, discontent, and regret intended to challenge you to use your power of choice to free yourself from your mediocre life. Your PI will encourage you to accept full responsibility for your life and make the life-changing choices necessary to pursue your ambitions and dreams.

What has your Potential Indicator been telling you these past few months or years? Has it been prompting and encouraging you to leave your comfort zone and step through your fears toward a preferred future? If this is the case, then it is time to give yourself permission:

permission to embrace and proactively pursue the realization of your true potential. This chapter will help you to do just that.

YOUR PERMISSION SLIP

Artist and author Vijali Hamilton writes, "We need to give ourselves permission to act out our dreams and visions. To live out our strongest dreams—even if it takes a lifetime." And your "permission slip" is your life-mission statement.

Self-help guru Stephen Covey writes, "Your mission statement is your written permission to do what is most important, most exciting to you." We started the process of creating this statement in chapter two, but will complete it in this chapter. When finished, this statement will be combined with your other work and incorporated into an action plan that will serve as your guide in the courageous life.

Thomas Edward Lawrence (of Arabia) said, "All men dream, but not equally. Those who dream by night in the dusty recesses of their minds, wake in the day to find it was vanity: but the dreamers of the day are dangerous men, for they act on their dreams with open eyes, to make them possible."

If you are reading this book, then you are one of those dangerous "dreamers of the day" who, with the help contained in these chapters, are preparing to step out toward a courageous life. Your life-mission statement will serve as the cornerstone from which your heroic dreams and goals will be carefully constructed and accomplished.

But before completing this work, let's review what you've done so far. We started off by asking the question, "What is your dream?" If you had the chance to tell your dream to a crowd of listeners, what would you say?

We then discussed how many individuals have chosen to bury, or ignore their dreams because of fear, doubt, and the belief that their "window of opportunity" to pursue their dreams has passed. But we also learned this is simply not true. It is never too late to uncover and pursue a dream.

In the second chapter we started the process of discerning what your dreams may be, and in the third chapter reviewed the science of the mind and the importance your thinking will play in successfully living out the courageous life. In addition, we surveyed your self-talk and listed the fears that have prevented you from pursuing your dreams in the past. Finally, in chapter four we continued the inner work of clarifying your personal values and strengths that will be used as you navigate the journey toward your dreams.

In this chapter we will finish the inner work started in previous chapters. Remember, your outward success will be directly influenced by the condition of your inner life, for as psychologist and philosopher William James wrote, "The greatest revolution of my life is the discovery that individuals can change the outer aspect of their lives by changing the inner attitudes of their minds."

WHAT IS A LIFE-MISSION STATEMENT?

Jack Canfield writes, "I believe each of us is born with a life purpose. Identifying, acknowledging, and honoring this purpose is perhaps the most important action successful people take." Best-selling author Dame Rebecca West adds, "It is the soul's duty to be loyal to its own desires. It must abandon itself to its master passion."

A life-mission statement addresses and clarifies the following questions:

❋ What do I want my life to represent?

❋ What is my master passion?

❋ Why do I exist?

❋ What do I want my life to stand for?

Your life-mission statement will be a clear and well-thought-out statement that will serve as your personal "creed." A creed is a formal statement of belief, derived from the Latin word, "credo," meaning "I believe." Various creeds have been written throughout the history of the Christian Church, for example, to help protect it from the false teachings of various individuals or sects; they set forth non-negotiable tenets of the faith.

But creeds are not only found in the religious community. Many professional communities have formed creeds that clearly articulate what that profession will fundamentally represent. For example, the Hippocratic Oath, to which many physicians adhere, is this type of creed. Such creeds state in clear terms what a person or profession believes and the standards that guide their behavior. Your life-mission statement will do the same for you. Your mission statement will state in very concise words what you want the central focus of your life to be.

I help coach the high-school football team in my hometown. In fact, right now, I am sitting next to the football field enjoying a lunch break between practices at a football camp we hold every June. Each year after the students get out of school for the summer, we take the team away for three days of camp where we review the basics of the game and introduce players to the offensive and defensive schemes that will be used during the regular season.

In June the weather is hot and humid, and though the coaches preach to the players that the heat should not be a big deal—it is *hot!* To make matters even more interesting, there's a water park about two hundred yards away from the field on which we practice, and the water slides and crystal-clear water in the pool are constantly beckoning us to come and jump in. Even I cannot help but give that cool blue water, with its adjacent concession stand, a yearning glance every once in a while.

So why do these young football players put up with long practices in the heat and humidity instead of enjoying the refreshing splash of the water park? Why do they choose to endure the sweat, soreness, and intense instruction from the coaches?

The answer is simple. These players and coaches are spurred on by an overarching team mission to, five months from now, win the con-

ference championship and give an all-out effort to win the state championship. Last season our team went 9-0 in the conference, and came
close to making it to the state championship game, and this year our
players want to continue the winning tradition. It is this overarching
mission that keeps us focused, positive and strong, despite the heat,
humidity . . . and water slide.

Your mission statement will do the same for you by giving your
life and daily activities a clear and uncompromising focus. This statement will also clarify what your deepest regret will be if you do *not*
choose to live the courageous life. It will clearly expose what will be
your biggest regret if you allow your fears and comfort zone to lure
you back into the mediocre life.

A life-mission statement is the first step in effectively leading yourself, and writing this personal creed should not be viewed as a piece of
creative writing, but rather an adventure in self-discovery in which you
are seeking to uncover your deepest passions, interests, and desires.
But before finishing the statement started in chapter two, let's review
in more detail the governing philosophy and motivation for having
such a statement.

First, a mission statement distinctly clarifies (in your own mind)
who you really are. Far too many individuals are living lives that have
been molded by the expectations of others. They are in careers others
thought would be "best"; are involved in activities their friends and
social group expect of them; many are living in houses, driving cars,
and buying clothes they cannot afford in an attempt to fit in.

A properly written mission statement can set a person free from
these burdensome expectations imposed by the world around them.
Acclaimed playwright and actor Harvey Fierstein writes, "Never be
bullied into silence. . . . Accept no one's definition of your life; define
yourself."

Far too many people are afraid to reveal who they really are to the
world, and as a result go through life wearing some type of mask, a
mask that not only hides their true selves but which presents a "face"
they hope will win them the acceptance of others. And while the mask

they are wearing may be smiling on the outside, their spirit is dying on the inside.

In his book *Discovering Your North Star,* leadership expert Ike Reighard writes that we all experience tremendous inner stress when we try to be somebody we are not, and this stress will never go away as long as we keep hiding our true identities behind whatever mask we have chosen to wear. (And whatever mask you try to wear eventually falls off anyway, exposing your true self for all to see.) The following is a list of "masks" a person may be tempted to hide behind:

❋ The mask of a hero, to cover up your fear of failure.

❋ The mask of a comedian, to hide your hurt and to divert attention from reality.

❋ The mask of someone completely in control, because you are terrified of being out of control.

❋ The mask of being a nice, accommodating person, because you want to avoid conflict at all costs.

❋ The mask of a caring person, because you hope this will win the appreciation of those you help.

❋ The mask of an incompetent slob, because nobody expects much from someone like that.

❋ The mask of a rebel, because it makes people admire you from a distance.

❋ The mask of rage, because you want people to be controlled by your anger.

❋ The mask of a shy, withdrawn person, because most people won't hurt somebody who is so fragile.

Super-salesman and motivational speaker Zig Ziglar writes, "I'm of the opinion that if you can't make it being yourself, you certainly can't make it being somebody else. It's OK to learn from others, even to discover some of the techniques or procedures they use in the process of becoming successful. But trying to be someone else really is hypocritical. Admire others; learn from others. But don't try to be somebody you're not."

Until I clarified my own mission statement, the opinions and expectations of others had too much influence over my life. I went into my career in engineering because it was what others thought I should do. It later took me two years to make a career change into youth ministry because that is what others said I should *not* do. I was initially a Minnesota Vikings football fan because my extended family was from Minnesota. I later became a Chicago Bears fan because a girl I liked in high school was a Bears fan. I even once remember tightly grasping a lit firecracker in my hand until it exploded because I wanted to wear the mask of a "tough" guy in front of my older brother and his friends. (Yes, I knew better—and yes, it did hurt.)

My question to you is, Who are you? Who are you . . . really? Someday when you lie on your deathbed, will people have known the real you? Taking the time to write your personal mission statement will help set you free to live the life for which you were created. It will help clarify the truth about yourself, and this truth will set you free!

A **second** reason why clarifying your life mission is beneficial is because it defines precisely where you should spend your time and energy. With laser precision, a life-mission statement helps to focus your life.

I have recently started to play golf. Many of my close friends love the game, so one of my new goals is to learn how to play with them. But since I am just starting out, I really don't have a clue what I'm doing. Last time out, I lost six golf balls. Three were hit into the water, and three others were driven so far off track, I couldn't find them, even after circling my golf cart a dozen times all around the fairway and those adjacent to it. I even managed to hit another golfer's ball, thinking it was mine! I still have a lot to learn.

But I have friends who are teaching me the game, and one thing I have learned is that the golf ball will fly off the tee in (usually) the same direction my feet are aligned. The placement of one's feet helps determine the direction the ball will fly (or roll, in my case) off the tee.

In the same way, your mission statement will set the direction of your life from here on out.

Once I finished writing my personal mission statement, my life started to change, and eventually it started to change drastically. I started evaluating various opportunities that came across my path in light of whether or not the opportunity would move me closer to accomplishing this mission.

With my purpose clarified, I now know exactly what type of activities I should spend my time and energy on and which activities I should steer away from. My life is focused. Now I have an effective evaluation tool to help determine if a certain activity is necessary and wise in light of my overall purpose in life.

Your mission statement will do the same for you.

Third, this work will strengthen your fortitude and resolve. Once you have clarified your mission in life, new and previously untapped energy resources will start to well up within, helping you overcome the barriers that will cross your path when pursuing a dream.

The life and accomplishments of Booker T. Washington provide a compelling example of how being clear regarding one's mission can create a powerful posture of fortitude and resolve. Booker T. Washington was an African American who grew up in the late 1800s, and it was his unfaltering dedication to his life mission that gave him the inner determination to overcome the numerous obstacles that all African Americans faced in those days. Fighting the stern prejudices of his time, coupled with little economic opportunity, Washington courageously pursued his mission.

Washington believed his calling was to "lay the foundation of the [African American] race through a generous education of the hand, head, and heart," and after persisting for many years, an opportunity to accomplish this mission was finally given to him. He recalled, "In May 1881 (. . .) in a way I dared not expect, the opportunity opened for me to begin my life work." It was then that he was invited to become the president of Tuskegee Institute, a small school for African Americans in Alabama. After taking this leadership role, Washington's life mission continued to provide him the stern stamina needed to confront the challenges of providing education to hundreds of African American youth, despite the lack of adequate facilities, funds, and equipment. Yet it was under his inspiring leadership that Tuskegee Institute grew from relative insignificance to eventually educating thousands of African Americans.

German philosopher Friedrich Nietzsche wrote that "a man can bear any *what* if he has a big enough *why.*" Booker T. Washington was committed to "generously" educating young African Americans, and this mission gave him the inner resolve to overcome numerous adversities he encountered along the way. In similar fashion, having a clear understanding of your life mission will release the stamina, determination, and perseverance needed as you step out to pursue your own unique calling.

The thought of starting my own consulting business entered my mind soon after I finalized my life-mission statement. Starting my own business would mean walking away from my current job, which proved a steady salary with benefits, into the unknown world of charging a fee for services I would provide. I had three children in grade school and the financial needs of my family were ongoing and growing. Nevertheless, I knew this was a journey on which I needed to embark. So after much prayer and planning, I resigned my job and started my own business.

Throughout this process, whenever I would begin to get cold feet, my life-mission statement would flow through my mind and encourage me to remain faithful. When clients were slow to pay, or business was sluggish, my life mission constantly stood beside me, encouraging me to press on and believe. But if I had not *first* taken the time to become crystal clear in my heart and mind regarding what I wanted my life to stand for, and the type of work I felt created to do, I would not have survived those difficult times. I do not believe I would have persevered.

A young man went to Socrates and asked how he could gain wisdom. Socrates replied by asking the young man to walk with him into a nearby lake. When the water got to be about four feet deep, Socrates suddenly grabbed the young man, pushed his head under the water, and then held it there. The young man thought it was a joke at first and did not resist. But as he was held under the water longer and longer, he became frantic. He struggled desperately to get free as his lungs burned for lack of oxygen. Finally, Socrates let him up, coughing, spluttering, and gasping for air. Socrates then said, "When you desire wisdom with the same intensity that you desire to breathe, then nothing will stop you from getting it."

It is the same with an inspiring mission. A compelling life mission will instill in you the strongest of desires to see it fulfilled. And when you combine your desires with steps of faith, nothing will be able to stop you from achieving it.

Finally, a mission statement will hold you accountable as you move into the future. The following story told by S. I. Kishor in the 1943 issue of *Collier's* magazine helps to illustrate this point:

> John Blanchard stood up from his bench, straightened his Army uniform and studied the crowd of people making their way through Grand Central Station in New York City. He was looking for the girl whose heart he knew, but whose face he had never seen.
>
> John Blanchard's interest in the young lady had begun thirteen months before in a used bookstore in Florida. Taking a book off the shelf, he found himself intrigued, not with the words of the book, but with the notes that were penciled in the margin. The soft handwriting reflected a thoughtful soul and insightful mind. In the front of the book he discovered the previous owner's name, Miss Hollis Maynell. He found that she lived in New York City. He wrote her a letter introducing himself and inviting her to correspond with him while he was overseas for service in World War II.

During the next thirteen months the two of them grew to know each other through the mail. A romance was budding. Blanchard requested a photograph, but she refused. She felt that if he really cared, it wouldn't matter what she looked like.

When the day finally came for him to return from Europe, they scheduled their first meeting—it was to be at 7:00 p.m. at the Grand Central Station in New York. "You'll recognize me," she wrote, "by the red rose I'll be wearing on my lapel." So at 7:00 he was in the station looking for a girl whose heart he loved, but whose face he had never seen. John Blanchard tells what happened in his diary . . .

"A young woman was coming toward me; her figure was lone and slim. Her blond hair lay back in curls from her delicate ears; her eyes were blue as flowers. Her lips and chin had a gentle firmness, and in her pale green suit she was like springtime come alive! I started toward her, entirely forgetting to notice that she was not wearing a rose. As I moved, a small, provocative smile cured her lips. 'Going my way sailor?' she murmured. Almost uncontrollably I made one step to go with her . . . and then I saw Miss Hollis Maynell.

"She was standing almost directly behind the girl. A woman well past forty, she had graying hair tucked under a worn hat . . . She was more than plump, her thick-ankled feet were thrust into low-heeled shoes. The girl in the green suit was walking quickly away, looking back at me.

"I felt as though I was split in two, so keen was my desire to follow the beautiful young lady, and yet so deep was my longing for the woman whose spirit had truly companioned me and upheld my own. And there she stood, wearing the red rose. Her pale, plump face was gentle and sensible; her gray eyes had a kindly twinkle. I did not hesitate. My fingers gripped that small, worn leather book that was to identify me to her. This would not be love, but it would be something precious, something perhaps even better than love, a friendship for which I would be forever grateful. I squared my shoulders, saluted and held out the book to the woman, even though while I spoke, I felt choked by the

bitterness of my disappointment. 'I'm Lieutenant John Blanchard, and you must be Miss Maynell. I am so glad you could
meet me; may I take you to dinner?' The woman's face broadened
into a tolerant smile. 'I don't know what this is about, son,' she
answered, 'but the young lady in the green suit who just went by,
she begged me to wear this rose on my coat. And she said if you
were to ask me out to dinner, I should go and tell you that she is
waiting for you in the big restaurant across the street. She said it
was some kind of test.'"

John Blanchard stayed focused on his "mission" to meet the female
friend who had nurtured and encouraged him through the experiences
of World War II. Though a conflicting desire strongly tempted him,
he chose not to allow this fleshly desire distract him from his overall
mission: to meet Miss Maynell. And the reward for staying aligned
with his mission forever exceeded the perceived benefits of wandering
away from it.

If you aren't careful, at times your desires and passions will flash
thoughts and goals into your mind that, if acted upon, will totally distract you from living out your purpose. But if you've taken time to
clarify your personal mission, it will help steer you away from any
alluring temptation that might conflict with what the true focus of
your life ought to be.

So How Does a Person Write a Life-Mission Statement?

Philosopher and mythologist Joseph Campbell describes the search for
meaning as the Hero's Journey. Campbell believes that self-transfor-
mation is a person's greatest challenge, and thus the Hero's Journey
begins when you are somehow awakened to the need for deep change
in your life. You may be awakened by an illumination, painful experience, or discomfort; whatever it is, the experience calls you to begin a
new adventure, an adventure in which you set out to align your life to
its true purpose. And though you may go through periods of doubt,

fear, and hardships along the way, at some point you will realize you have succeeded in completing the Hero's Journey and your life and purpose have become one.

Unfortunately, many people choose to never embrace the Hero's Journey. They never turn onto the hero's path because they "feel too busy to search for meaning. . . . Instead, they sleepwalk through life, operating on automatic pilot most of the time. They meet their obligations but rarely question whether they could be reaching for something more." (*The Power of Full Engagement,* by Jim Loehr and Tony Schwartz)

What follows are some simple exercises that will help you turn onto the Hero's Journey by clarifying your unique mission. Get away to some quiet place where you can focus and think as you work through the following exercises. Again, the first statement you write will only be an initial draft that will be revised and reworded for the next few months until you know in your spirit you have a life-mission statement that synergizes your heart and mind.

To get started, answer ten questions adapted from the book *The Power of Focus,* by Jack Canfield that will assess if your life is presently (and actively) centered on a core mission. Simply mark "yes," "don't know/not sure," or "no."

1. **Do you confidently know what specific activities you are good at, and which ones energize you?**

   ____ *Yes*   ____ *Don't know/Not sure*   ____ *No*

2. **Do you fully and regularly utilize your most-enjoyed skill or talent?**

   ____ *Yes*   ____ *Don't know/Not sure*   ____ *No*

3. **Does your daily work further some interest or issue that you deeply care about?**

   ____ *Yes*   ____ *Don't know/Not sure*   ____ *No*

4. Do you see yourself, through your work, making a difference in the world?

____ Yes   ____ Don't know/Not sure   ____ No

5. Do you look forward to most days with a sense of enthusiasm?

____ Yes   ____ Don't know/Not sure   ____ No

6. Have you clearly developed, and articulated, your own philosophy of life, or life mission?

____ Yes   ____ Don't know/Not sure   ____ No

7. Are you being bold and taking the necessary risks to live out your life mission?

____ Yes   ____ Don't know/Not sure   ____ No

8. Do you feel a sense of meaning and purpose in your life?

____ Yes   ____ Don't know/Not sure   ____ No

9. Do you have written and specific goals to help you pursue your life mission?

____ Yes   ____ Don't know/Not sure   ____ No

10. Are you living your life to the fullest now, instead of hoping that things will work out someday?

____ Yes   ____ Don't know/Not sure   ____ No

Score the results as follows:

For each "Yes" answer give yourself a zero (0)

"Don't know/Not sure" scores a one (1)

Each "No" answer scores a two (2)

These questions are subjective; however, they indicate how clearly you have articulated your life mission in your mind, and how well you have aligned your life to that mission.

If you scored between zero and six, your life is pretty focused. You have a sense of direction and are intent on making your life mission a reality.

If you scored between seven and thirteen, you may have a *sense* of purpose for your life, but need to further clarify what it is and make further choices to align your life to that mission.

If you scored between thirteen and twenty, you are running the risk of not reaching your potential and living a mediocre life. But be encouraged, the fact you are reading this book, and applying its lessons, will very quickly move you up on the scale.

As I said earlier, a life-mission statement is the first step in effectively leading yourself, and is an adventure of self-discovery in which you uncover your passions, interests, and deepest desires that otherwise may have remained buried. In addition, because every individual is unique, your life-mission statement will reflect your uniqueness, both in content and form.

Writing a statement of this magnitude and importance will not be done overnight. It will take deep introspection, careful analysis, thoughtful expression, and many rewrites to produce something in final form. The following exercises will help you walk through that process.

THE DAY AFTER YOUR LAST DAY

It's time to search your soul. An effective way to begin the process of formulating your life-mission statement is to begin with the end of your life in mind. This will help you focus on what you want to be (character), what you want to do (contribution and achievement), and the values or principles upon which being and doing are based.

To do this, picture yourself at your own funeral service. On a sheet of paper, record the impressions you have in this funeral visualization. What would you like the people at your funeral to say about your life? What contributions, what achievements would you want them to remember? Look at the people around you. What difference would you like to have made in their lives? Take time to write your impressions in your journal.

To explore these issues even more deeply, reflect on the following statements and questions:

- Take a few moments to write down your current roles in life (spouse, parent, worker, friend, etc.). If your life continues as it is, at the end of your life will you be satisfied with how you fulfilled these various roles? Why or why not?

- Write your response to the questions: What is the meaning and a purpose to my existence? How can I maximize my life's journey? What are my skills and strengths? Passions? Interests?

- Write out your first draft of a life-mission statement. Daily revise for the next ten days. The goal is to keep this statement to one or two sentences—or three at the most—so it can be easily memorized, internalized, and remembered.

THE JOURNEY

This exercise is adapted from the book *The Journey,* in which author Arnold Patent provides the following process to clarify one's mission:

1. List two of your unique personal qualities (such as *enthusiasm* and *creativity*).

2. List one or two ways you enjoy expressing those qualities when interacting with others (such as *to support* and *to inspire*).

3. Assume the world is perfect right now. What does this world look like? How is everyone interacting with everyone else? What does it feel like? Write your answer as a statement, in the present tense, describing the ultimate condition, the perfect world as you see it and feel it. Remember, a perfect world is a fun place to be.

   Example: Everyone is freely expressing his own unique talents. Everyone is working in harmony. Everyone is expressing love.

4. Combine the three prior points into a single statement.

   Example: My purpose is to use my creativity and enthusiasm to support and inspire others to freely express their talents in a harmonious and loving way.

INQUIRE WITHIN

Author Jack Canfield provides a simple approach to clarifying your overall life mission. After you have relaxed yourself and are in a peaceful state, ask yourself, *What is my purpose for living?* and *What is my unique role in the universe?* Allow the answer to simply come to you. Let it be as expansive as you can imagine. Do not limit yourself. The words that come to you do not need to be flowery or poetic; what is important is how inspired the words make you feel.

In addition, motivational author Stephen Covey offers the following reflective questions:

- What are three things you would do if you knew you could not fail?

- Take a minute to think about the last time you were really energized about life . . . what were you doing and who were you with?

- Imagine yourself on an epic journey, with you as the hero or heroine of the story. What do you imagine your journey to be about? Describe what you are doing, who is it for, why you are doing it, and what it results in.

- Think about the major events, accomplishments, challenges, and successes you have experienced in your lifetime. If you had the power to turn back time, what would you change?

- As you reflect over the events of your life, what are you most proud of?

- If you were given ten million dollars and had to give it all to charity, which charity would it be given to, and how would you wish the funds to be used?

The following are sample life-mission statements provided as examples:

- "My life purpose is to reach, and mentor others to reach, our highest potential while keeping life in balance."

- "To help as many people as I can during my lifetime, in a way that significantly improves their lives."

- "In my roles as a husband, father, and financial services expert, my mission is to reflect trust, honesty, love, and integrity in all my care and service. I am committed to providing my family and friends with my priority attention and time, while also providing my clients with expert and successful financial solutions that are tailored to their particular needs and goals."

- "Throughout each day in my life I strive to be loyal to my friends and family, lead a successful career that I will enjoy, stay healthy, and take on any challenges that come my way."

- "My mission is to provide love, support, coaching, and encouragement to my family and those in my business in order for them to realize their full potential and live safe, highly productive, balanced, economically successful lives."

FIRST DRAFT OF MY LIFE-MISSION STATEMENT:

_____

_____

_____

_____

_____

_____

Good job! Hopefully, you now have a solid first draft of your life-mission statement. As you continue to reflect on this statement, keep the following four guiding thoughts in mind.

1 It is up to you

Viktor Frankl wrote, "Everyone has his own specific vocation or mission in life to carry out. A concrete assignment that demands fulfillment. Therein he cannot be replaced, nor can his life be repeated. Thus, everyone's task is unique as is his specific opportunity to implement it."

Though others may be invited to help formulate your mission statement and corresponding list of dreams, ultimately this inner work must be completed by you. Just as another person cannot give you your dreams, or hand you your future, so no one will be able to tell you what your overall mission in life should be. This is something you will need to discover on your own.

Dreamers are also very clear thinkers. Effective dreamers have developed the personal discipline to consistently assess their lives and determine where adjustments need to be made so they can continue moving toward their dreams.

As a consultant, part of my job is to force my clients to *think*. Many individuals are so caught up in the rat race of their schedules and careers that they are living a reactive life. They are reacting to the demands of their schedules, family, clients, coworkers, and anything else that happens to come along. But those who effectively live out the courageous life are careful to own each day. They take time, on a regular basis, to reflect on what is going well, and what areas of life still need improvement.

Remember, "There is a choice you have to make in everything you do. So keep in mind that in the end, the choice you make, makes you." (Anonymous) So far, you have been asked to do some important inner work before stepping out to pursue your courageous dreams.

Have you taken the time to get away and start this work? If so, great job! You have chosen wisely. If not, I encourage you to own your life by choosing to do the important work outlined thus far, for no one can determine your overall mission and dreams for you. Own your life by taking the responsibility to decide what your future will look like.

2 A life-mission statement does not have to be grandiose to be effective

Your statement does not have to be one that will change the world; it just needs to impact *your* world. The purpose of your life is to live a life of purpose, not to become famous, rich, or popular. A successful life is one where you first clarify your unique calling, and then proactively set out to see that mission realized. Don't put pressure on yourself to create some grandiose life mission for yourself . . . just take the time to honestly discern *your* life calling, and then focus on taking the steps necessary to actively live out that specific calling.

My mission is to help people reach their full potential in ways that respect a balanced life and honor their Creator. I am not sure how grand this life calling is . . . but it is what it is. And it is big enough for me. It keeps me true to myself and to who I was meant to be.

3 Create your future from your future, not your past

You have hurts and pains from your past. You may have gone through very trying times, including health issues, abuse, divorce, death of close relatives or friends, or unwise choices that have caused hardship or pain.

Sometimes when a person goes through the process of discerning her mission in life, she starts to recall failures and pains from the past and questions if she has what it takes to live the courageous life at all.

We're all flawed in some way. I personally struggle with pain resulting from choices in my past and my failure to live up to my expectations of how a spiritual man, husband, father, and friend should behave. I've got plenty of clubs from my past that I could use to thoroughly beat my life purpose and dreams out of me . . . if I chose to do so. And you could do the same with clubs from your own past.

The Apostle Paul wrote, "But one thing I do: Forgetting what is behind and straining toward what is ahead, I press on toward the goal to win the prize for which God has called me . . . All of us who are mature should take such a view of things."

Don't let the past limit your future. Instead, forget what is behind and choose to press on toward the goal. Embrace your dreams and choose to believe in yourself and the future. Remember that "if you believe you are too small to have an impact, try going to bed with a mosquito in the room." (Anita Koddick)

4 Change happens

Motivational author Stephen Covey writes that there are only three constants in life: change, principles, and choice. There's a good chance that as you grow and journey through various seasons of life, your life mission and dreams will change and need to be revised. This is OK, normal, and to be expected.

Early in my life, when I was about one year old, my mission in life was to eat food and chew on anything I could fit in my mouth. It was a simple yet often frustrating mission. Later, when I was about three years old, my mission changed to increase my personal possessions of candy and toys. It was this obsession that ushered in my deep appreciation for Halloween, Christmas, birthdays, and even Easter (which provided lesser quantities of jelly beans and chocolate eggs).

At about seven years of age, my mission in life revolved around continuing to increase my quantity of toys and candy, riding my bike around town, and looking for treasure in abandoned gold mines with my father in the mountains of Colorado. Then, in my teen years, my life calling turned to sports, junk food, friends, and a brown-eyed girl. And I could go on.

Life brings change. It brings change physically, emotionally, socially, and spiritually, while also ushering changes in your personal values, priorities, skills, and dreams. Although I believe a person's life mission will likely remain somewhat consistent after he reaches his adult years, don't be surprised if there are changes of emphasis and focus as the years go by. But if you have developed the *habit* of reflective thinking, you'll be able to sense these shifts in your spirit and make the necessary adjustments. Again, dreamers are effective thinkers.

While your overall mission *may* change somewhat over the years, your dreams and goals will *definitely* undergo revision. For example, once I have finished the dream of writing this book, I will need to move on to the next dream. Though I know my next dream will need to align with my mission, values, and unique strengths, I am still pondering what that dream will be.

The courageous life is a lifelong journey. When you achieve one dream, your mind and spirit will push you on to the next. You see, you can never actually reach your full potential because as you grow, so does your capacity and potential to do more. So as you travel through life, celebrate your accomplishments, but also maintain the critical habit of getting alone by yourself on a consistent basis to reflect, think, and hear what your heart is telling you. It will prompt you when it is time once again to step away from your comfort zone and embrace a new dream.

Time to move on

In the next chapter you'll pull together all the inner work you have done and create a plan that will serve as a guide as you move outward toward your courageous dreams. We have finished the work of clarifying your values, strengths, and life mission and are now ready to take the list of dreams you have been working on and incorporate them into a personal action plan to assist you as you step out on a new path leading to your dreams!

CHAPTER 6

What Is Your Real Job?

"I wish to work miracles . . ."
—Leonardo da Vinci

I remember anticipating the day I would graduate from college and start my first "real" job—when I would finish my studies in engineering and be set free to do what I had been trained to do, while making good money and enjoying the rewards of a new career. Each exam during college made me yearn for that day more and more. But after entering my new profession as an engineer, it was not long before I sensed there was still something missing. Even though I enjoyed the people I worked with, for some reason my "real" job was not as satisfying as I imagined it would be.

Something was just not right.

It was not until later that I realized my goal coming out of college was too small. Back then, my aim was to get into a well-paying engineering career, where I would work hard for the next forty years and then walk away with a good retirement package when I was sixty-five. Then, in retirement, I'd be able to do whatever I wanted to do.

I now realize this goal of finding a job, with good pay and benefits, was not a wise ambition. What I lacked was an acute awareness of my dreams and an understanding of how my dreams were meant to be expressed in my everyday life and career. It took too long to figure out that my real job in life is *not* to find a well-paying and secure occupation—but my real job in life is to pursue my dreams.

And the same is true for you. Your real job in life is to pursue your courageous dreams. Anything less will only leave you with underlying feelings of frustration and regret.

Stephen Covey uses an interesting term called "secondary greatness" to describe people who are successful in society's eyes, yet are living lives, and are in careers, which leave them personally unfulfilled and dissatisfied. These individuals may appear successful on the outside, but they are unmotivated and discontent on the inside. And while they may have been extremely energized and motivated early on in their lives and careers, they have now come to a point where they know something is missing.

In many cases, what is missing are their courageous dreams. As they have climbed the ladder of success, they now realize their ladders are leaning against the wrong wall—against a wall that, though providing financial security, will not allow them to fulfill their ultimate callings in life. This is a problem.

It is at this point these individuals are faced with a gut-wrenching choice. They are forced to choose between remaining on their current ladder, or making the necessary changes to rearrange their life to strategically include their dreams—where they take steps to align "what they do" with "who they are." These are the types of bold choices that form the foundation of the courageous life.

MY CHALLENGE FOR YOU

My challenge for you is to eventually come to the point where you are not only pursuing your dreams, but your dreams and career become one. This is possible in many cases. While your level of income may or may not remain the same as in your previous career, whatever the financial difference, at the end of your life you will consider any price you paid a real bargain.

It is a worthy ambition to live the type of courageous life role modeled by the likes of Leonardo da Vinci, Joan of Arc, Christopher Columbus, Abraham Lincoln, Thomas Edison, Mother Teresa, Margaret Thatcher, Billy Graham, Ronald Reagan, Bill Clinton, and a handful of people around us who have made the proactive choice to align their professions with their dreams.

While this may not be easy to accomplish, and will certainly call for courageous steps of faith along the way, the life stories of others who have already completed this daring quest should encourage us as we step out to do the same. Publisher and millionaire Malcolm Forbes said, "The biggest mistake people make in life is not trying to make a living at doing what they enjoy the most."

One example of a person who strategically aligned his work to a dream was Leonardo da Vinci. His dream was "to work miracles," and in many ways, da Vinci did just that. Born in 1452, and living to the age of sixty-two, Leonardo, the artist, helped transform the direction of art. His *Mona Lisa* and *The Last Supper* are universally recognized as two of the greatest paintings ever produced. Leonardo was also a renowned architect, sculptor, and inventor. During his life he made plans for a flying machine, a helicopter, a parachute, and many other marvels, including an extendable ladder, three-speed transmission, a machine for cutting treads in screws, the bicycle, an adjustable wrench, snorkel, hydraulic jack, the world's first revolving stage, locks for a canal system, folding furniture, a water-powered alarm clock, and a crane for clearing ditches. He also made plans for weapons that would be deployed four hundred years later, including the armored tank, machine gun, mortar, guided missile, and the submarine. Leonardo lived out his dream to invent many miracles of art and science, and he did so by making that dream his career.

My challenge is to view the courageous life as your real job, plain and simple. And though you may need a second job to pay your bills for a while, I encourage you to make this a permanent shift in your thinking by embracing by faith what is in your heart. If you do, in time you will realize that the two have become one—that your dream has become your full-time career as well! Epictetus wrote, "First say to yourself what you would be; and then do what you have to do."

THE GUIDE TO YOUR DREAMS

We are now ready to pull together all your work from the previous chapter and create a tool that will serve as your guide on this courageous journey . . . your personalized action plan.

But, first, why is an action plan needed at all? How will the action plan help move you toward your dreams and goals? The late management consultant Peter Drucker wrote, "In a few hundred years, when the history of our time is written from a long-term perspective, it is likely the most important event those historians will see is not technology, not the Internet, not e-commerce. It is an unprecedented change in the human condition. For the first time—literally—substantial and rapidly growing numbers of people have choices. For the first time, they will have to manage themselves . . . and society is totally unprepared for it."

The reason an action plan is of critical importance is because each day we are faced with a growing number of choices, opinions, and distractions. We live at a time when, if you are going to pursue your dreams, you'll need to lead yourself very wisely and efficiently. A well-prepared action plan will help you do just that.

THE BALANCED LIFE

Having read this far, you know I am a big believer in courageously pursuing one's dreams and goals. But I am just as adamant that those dreams should be pursued in a way that does *not* compromise other areas of your life: you pursue your dreams with those you love, not at the expense of those you love; reach your potential with your health, not at the expense of your health; and achieve your heroic ambitions while staying connected with your spiritual center, and not at the expense of your faith. I could go on, but you get the point.

The core philosophy of the personalized action plan is to help you reach your potential and dreams while *also* living a balanced and healthy life. Individuals who are the most successful are those who excel, not only in their careers, but in multiple areas of their lives as well. These people effectively accomplish the difficult task of keeping the various dimensions of life (including work, family, social, spiritual, emotional, and physical lives) not only balanced but growing. They are simultaneously growing in their ability to remain spiritually centered and aware, socially balanced and interconnected, physically healthy and vibrant, and emotionally strong and nurtured.

As you may suspect, this is not an easy task.

Your life can easily drift out of balance, where you start to focus too much, and for too long, on one dimension of your life at the expense of other areas. For example, I have had the tendency to become slightly addicted to various television shows over the course of my life. In high school (during the late '70s) the TV series I was hooked on was *M*A*S*H,* then it was *The Love Boat,* later it was *WKRP in Cincinnati,* only to be followed by *Magnum, P.I.; L.A. Law; Seinfeld;* and a few others . . . finally landing on my favorite current show *The Office.* The era of cable television doesn't help either. In the '70s and early '80s, my favorite show would be shown once a week, but now with cable television, programs like *The Office* can be seen up to two or three times a day.

This is not good, for if I am not careful, I could easily allow cable television, and my personal collection of shows on DVD distract me from my family, friends, and faith, all of which I value much more highly than any television series or DVD collection.

I have a good friend who has chosen to not install cable television in his home because he is self-aware enough to know that if he did, he would soon become addicted to the Weather Channel. He knows himself well enough to understand that if available in his house, he would spend too much time watching the weather, and related shows, at the expense of spending time with his family and pursuing the dream of starting his own business. Instead, he limits his obsession by volunteering one morning a week as the weather DJ at a local public radio station—and by chasing tornadoes when they happen to pass through central Illinois!

Many people allow excessive attention to their jobs lure them away from paying adequate attention to the other dimensions of life. The desire to succeed in their careers slowly starts to distract them from their families, physical and spiritual health, and the pursuit of hobbies and friendships. In many cases, the lives of these individuals can remain out of balance for too many years, resulting in the loss of their marriages, health, and respect of their children. "What good will it be for a man if he gains the whole world, yet forfeits his soul?" asks the Christian Bible; we could add "and forfeits his family, health, integrity, friends, and dreams in the process?"

We all know individuals who have lived this type of life, for there are many to be found in corporate America. I personally know a man who lost his wife, children, and many friends because for years he was obsessed with his career and business. For most of his career he was too distracted to relationally connect with those he loved, and who loved him.

Now in his mid-fifties, he is alone, his health is average at best, and he has few quality relationships. Twenty years ago he was married, had a great family, was financially successful, and was a leader in his church and community. Today, because he was not careful to live a balanced life, he has almost lost everything—except the one thing he did focus on during those years: his job.

He still has his high-level corporate job.

If you pursue your dreams in a way that ignores other areas of life, you will never reach your full potential. The scars and pain from years of neglect will demand too high a toll. Yet this does not have to be the case. The first step to maintaining balance is to understand why people allow their lives to drift out of balance in the first place. Though the causes are many, the following five reasons are near the top of the list:

A person does not value balance in her life

We protect and nurture what we value, and neglect what we place little importance on. You may recall back in chapter four that "life balance" was on my list of personal values. But the proof that I value balance is not because it is on some list; the evidence will be apparent in my daily behavior, in what I actually do with my time and energy, day in and day out.

Your behavior *always* reveals your true intent. We can try to make ourselves feel good by listing a specific priority (like faith, family, integrity, life balance, physical fitness . . .) on your list of values, but it will be your daily behavior that will prove whether you truly intend to live out that value. If your values are not reflected in your daily behaviors, then you're only paying lip service to that issue in your life.

For example, if I state that having an intimate relationship with my wife and children is a value of mine, the proof will be reflected in my daily behavior . . . or not. Do I actually carve out time each day and week to spend quality time with my family? Would my wife and others close to me say my actions reflect this value? Would my children say my behavior consistently reflects this stated value of mine?

If they answer yes, then my actions give proof to that value. If they answer with a no, then it would be correct to conclude that intimacy with my family is *not* a value of mine, for when I make choices regarding my time, something else is winning out.

No one should ever be too impressed when someone proclaims that a certain priority is included on his or her personal list of values. What *should* be impressive is when that value is consistently reflected in that person's behavior.

If a person declares he has decided to live a physically fit life by adjusting his diet and exercise, the evidence will be found in that person's actions. If in subsequent days and months he starts to eat healthily and sets aside time to exercise consistently, then his behavior proves he intends to stay physically fit.

But if, after a few weeks or months, he's quit working out and can be seen sneaking away to McDonald's to visit his old friend "Mr. Big Mac" and *his* friend "Mr. Super-Size It," then we know that staying physically fit is not his true intent. He actually wants something else, something more. What he possibly really desires is the freedom to eat what he wants, whenever he wants. Or maybe he values sleeping in each morning, instead of getting out of bed to exercise before heading off to work. Or possibly this individual wants to stay physically fit only if he doesn't have to run in the heat, rain, humidity, against the wind, up a hill, or in any way that causes him to sweat.

The point is that there's something this individual wants more than living a physically fit life. And though the truth may be hard to admit, if he'll admit the truth, he can then take this understanding and begin to change the way he thinks about his health. This will in turn change his actions, for as we learned in chapter three, you change your life by first changing the way you think, for "as a man thinks in his heart, so is he."

Your actions do speak much louder than your words. If you say you value living a balanced life, then the proof will be in your daily behaviors.

Living a reactive versus a proactive life

The second reason people's lives get out of balance, and even out of control, is they are *reacting* to life instead of *proactively* choosing how they will live each day.

No one can live a balanced life, much less the courageous life, if she doesn't exert complete control over how she spends her time and energy. Remember the quote by Peter Drucker, "For the first time— literally—substantial and rapidly growing numbers of people have choices. For the first time, they will have to manage themselves . . . and society is totally unprepared for it."

One reason people and families are living lives that are on the verge of being out of control is that society provides a vast number of "good" activities to be involved in: sport teams, band, dance lessons, camps, leagues, church activities . . . There are so many good choices available that families feel overwhelmed, and pressured to fit all (or most) of them into their weekly schedules. As a result, they are busy almost every night of the week attending various sporting, church or synagogue, club, and other related events, leaving virtually no spare time in their schedule and no spare energy in their tank.

You must remember that you always have a choice. You are never a victim of your schedule, or anything else for that matter. Prominent CEO and author W. Clement Stone wrote, "You always do what you want to do. This is true with every act. You may say you had to do something, or that you were forced to, but actually, whatever you do, you do by choice." And Stephen Covey writes, "Any time you think the problem is out there, that very thought is the problem." You always have the ability to choose your way, and it is wisely using your power of choice that will set you free from living a reactive life—no matter what society throws your way.

I am aware that this isn't easy. We have three children who are all very active, and if allowed, the demands of school, sports, camps, and church functions would squeeze every bit of family time out of our schedule. But as parents, my wife and I are careful to protect our family life and priorities by making choices to limit what we, and our teenagers, are involved in. We've chosen to not surrender our family vacations, family nights out, or other matters of family life to the school system, local sporting activities, or even our church.

Now understand, all three of our children are active in church, school, athletics, and other extracurricular activities, and I help coach the football team at my son's high school, but we have also set firm boundaries that limit the extent of these activities. And while we have experienced some push-back from our children, and in rare cases from coaches and other leaders, this is ground we will not surrender.

Embrace the power of choice, and forever eliminate a victim mentality from your thinking. Be willing to go against the flow and courageously choose the life *you* want for yourself and your family, a life that reflects *your* values and moves you toward *your* dreams.

Lack of feedback or awareness

As you pursue the courageous life you must remember that you are blind. You are partially blind to who you really are. And since you don't see yourself for who you really are, you need to continuously seek the wisdom and perspective of individuals who know you very well. There will be times when you don't realize that your life is getting out of balance. And though you may not recognize this, those around you will.

There have been times when I believed I was balancing my work and family quite well, only to later find out that my wife or children were feeling neglected. And though I may not have been aware this was happening, it was the feedback from my family that helped get me back on course. But there are other useful sources of feedback as well.

For example, there is the weight scale in the bathroom. Whenever I try to convince myself that I am immune to foods with a high content of sugar, or think I can go a couple of weeks without working out, the scale in my bathroom is quick to correct my thinking. My point is, whenever your life starts to drift out of balance, it will send signals intended to help you get back on track. But these signals will only help if you look for, and then embrace, the feedback sent your way.

I mentioned in chapter four that I have a love-hate relationship with the concept of feedback. Though I value the theory of feedback, I have a natural tendency to believe I am already perfect, or that others don't notice my faults.

And I know I'm not alone in this. It's been my experience as a consultant that many leaders struggle with receiving feedback from their peers or subordinates without becoming defensive and personally upset by what is said. The reason for this is pride. Pride prevents you from humbly seeking and accepting what others see in your life. But since you are blind to yourself in some areas, the seeds for your future growth and success will always be found in the feedback being sent to you from these various sources. Feedback really is the breakfast of champions.

To live the courageous life, one needs to have the fortitude to ask courageous questions. I challenge you to embrace the concept of feedback and find out what other people think about your life. How would your subordinates, close friends, and spouse rate the balance in your life? And when you receive the feedback, look for patterns and themes. If one person says you are an elephant, they are probably delusional, but if three or four people say you are an elephant . . . then, in some odd way, you are an elephant. Accept what other people observe in your life and resist the temptation to be defensive by simply thanking them for their honesty.

Lack of self-discipline

A fourth reason an individual's life may be out of balance is that she hasn't developed the two fundamental qualities found in almost everyone who is a self-made success: self-discipline and self-control.

Self-discipline is "the systematic, willing, and purposeful action taken each day, which leads one toward the completion of their self-assigned goals." Self-control is "the systematic, willing, and purposeful action taken each day, which leads one to effectively suppress and replace lesser desires for those which reflect the highest virtues of character, integrity, love, and service." (Jack Canfield)

Self-discipline allows a person to exhibit the positive behaviors needed to keep her moving toward her dreams, while self-control keeps negative influences from hindering the progress she's making. Like the positive and negative poles of a magnet, both are needed to move a person forward in the courageous life.

There are a significant number of people who really want to live a healthy and balanced life, yet simply do not get it done. Why? For many, the problem lies in their habitual inability to exert self-discipline and self-control in their lives. They have made choices and then developed habits that make it very difficult to control and effectively manage their appetites, moods, and passions.

American society is very self-indulgent. Whenever I walk through the local shopping mall, my lusts and appetites commence an all-out war against my self-discipline and self-control. I walk by the ice cream shop and desire three scoops of mint chocolate chip ice cream. Half an hour later, when the ice cream is gone, I start to covet a salted pretzel with some of that hot cheese all over it. Then, as I walk past one of my favorite clothing stores, I imagine myself in a new shirt or two. And then leave it to Victoria's Secret to tempt me to buy a few gifts for my wife.

As I walk through that mall, my passions and desires conduct an all-out war to entice me to give in to all that is abundantly offered. And I will be honest, there are times when my self-discipline and control win, and there are other times when I walk out of the mall carrying too many bags of "stuff," while also feeling nauseated from too much ice cream, pretzels, and those big gumballs you can buy for a quarter.

If you are going to live a healthy and balanced life, you need to believe that living a disciplined life will, in the end, provide more satisfaction than giving into your vices and lusts. Though not easy, a self-disciplined life sets you free to pursue your courageous dreams, while also protecting the areas of your life you hold *most* dear.

And don't kid yourself, there are many people who think they are self-disciplined and controlled, yet are fooling themselves. They are still overweight, spend too little time with their spouses and children, feel disconnected spiritually, are drifting away from their friends, and/or are making only modest (if any) progress toward their dreams and goals. Though they think they are exhibiting self-control and personal discipline, the fruit of their lives proves otherwise.

Many individuals are addicted to the pleasures of life. And this addiction is distracting them from the courageous life, while causing their dreams and goals to remain dormant. And though currently anesthetized by the pleasures of the world, one day they will wake up and realize that these tempting indulgences have only left them with feelings of regret and remorse over what could have been. They will reflect back and mourn the years that have been lost.

Embracing a life of self-discipline and self-control leads to a *very* large payoff. But this payoff is never immediate. Belief and patience through the days, months, and years will be necessary.

Don't know how

Finally, many individuals are not living a balanced life because they just do not know what a balanced life looks like, or how to live in a balanced way. Having already discussed what a balanced life is, and why living in balance is important, I now want to mention a few practical ways *how* a person can start to establish balance in his life:

1. The *first* step is to make the cognitive choice to value a life where you actively grow in each of the various dimensions of life, while *also* stepping out toward your dreams. To make the choice not only to value this kind of life, but to actually start living such a life. This is where the rubber hits the road. To live a balanced life, we must be willing to take one hundred percent responsibility for everything we do. Remember, "Your life is not a coincidence. It is a direct reflection of your choices." A balanced life begins when we make the choice to leave old habits that limit your potential and form new habits that will accelerate your growth.

2. The *second* step is to take a few minutes to assess how balanced your life is now. Remember that one of the building blocks of success and significance is to take time on a regular basis to grow in your self-awareness—to "know thyself" better and more completely. Throughout history, self-knowledge has gone hand in hand with inner happiness and outward success because to perform at your best you need to know both *who* you are and *why* you think and feel the way you do. In regards to living a balance life, the following five questions will help you do just that:

     What does a balanced life look like for you at your stage in life?

     What does it look like when your life is out of balance?

     What tends to get your life out of balance?

✳ What are the essentials you will need to embrace, or change, to get your life back in balance?

✳ What will it take to get you there?

3. The *third* step is to list the various dimensions of your life and determine how you specifically want to grow in each of these areas over the next few months and years. In this step you are deciding exactly what you want each area of your life to look like in the future. Best-selling author Brian Tracy writes, "All great achievement begins with your deciding what it is you really want and then dedicating yourself wholeheartedly to attaining it." Actor and author Ben Stein writes, "The indispensable first step to getting the things you want out of life is this: decide what you want."

Later in this chapter we will work through a process to help you do this. You will clarify the various dimensions of your life and start listing specific goals for each area. We will then combine these goals with your list of dreams and incorporate them into an action plan.

In the remaining pages, we're going to discuss the difference between courageous dreams and goals; discuss the process of how to effectively set goals; and then create a first draft of an action plan to guide you in the courageous life. Here's where we finally pull together all the work you have completed and craft a tool that will serve as your guide as you step away from your comfort zone and courageously venture out toward your dreams!

DREAMS VERSUS GOALS

All through this book I have used the terms *dreams* and *goals*. Though they are similar, your dreams and goals will fill different and distinct roles in the action plan we will create. For your purposes, and in combination with your "life-mission statement," here is how your dreams and goals will be defined and used (an example is provided at the end of this chapter):

* Your life-mission statement will serve as your "grand life dream" or "grand mission." This overarching statement (which you wrote in the last chapter) briefly states what you want your life to be about and stand for. This statement will set the overall course of your life and be the grand measuring stick used to ensure that your dreams and goals are aligned with your calling in life.

* Your courageous dream will serve as the single and significant goal on which you are *currently* focusing, which will enable you to actively live out your life mission. Though you will have a list of various dreams you're considering, your *courageous dream* will be the *one* you choose to pursue for now. As I mentioned earlier, one of my first courageous dreams was to start my own leadership consulting business. After that was completed, my next courageous dream was to write this book. And after completing this book, I will move on to the next dream that will allow me to live out my mission in life.

* Your *goals* will be a list of specific goals you create under *each* of the various dimensions in your life. This list of goals will ensure you're keeping your life in balance and that each dimension of your life is growing as you pursue your courageous dream(s).

Your *life-mission statement, courageous dreams,* and *goals* will form what I firmly believe is your "real job." In this arrangement, your life-mission statement will set the overall course and direction of your life. Your courageous dream(s) will define the specific grand pursuit you believe is right for your life. And then your specific goals will help ensure that you're pursuing the courageous life *with* your relationships, health, faith, emotions . . . not at the *expense* of these in your life.

Creating your initial list of goals

You will soon make a first draft of goals for each dimension of your life, but before doing this, let's briefly review why setting specific goals is important in the first place.

JC Penney said, "Give me a stock clerk with a goal and I'll give you a man who will make history. But give me a man without a goal, and I will give you a stock clerk." The Christian Bible says that "without a vision the people will perish." Whether it is an individual, organization, or an entire nation, if that entity does not have clearly defined and energizing goals, it will not be able to sustain its existence, or reach its full potential. Self-help author Michael Kiefer writes, "No goals, no future." Clearly defined goals can provide the fuel to reignite a life, an organization, or the heart of an entire nation.

One of the most powerful examples of a goal that inspired an entire nation, sparking the imagination and energy of millions of people for nearly a decade, was a goal articulated in 1960 when President John F. Kennedy declared that the United States of America would put a man on the moon by the end of the decade. This audacious vision succeeded in synergizing an entire nation for nearly ten years. And despite enormous obstacles, setbacks, and challenges, the goal was reached on July 21, 1969, when astronaut Neil Armstrong took his first steps on the dusty, gray surface of the moon. That event will forever be one of the proudest days in the history of the United States.

This same type of compelling vision is critically needed in your personal life as well, for without clearly defined goals, your life will quickly drift into a mediocre, tedious, and unfulfilling existence. "In the absence of clearly defined goals, we become strangely loyal to performing daily acts of trivia." (Author unknown)

Ask those nearing the end of their life and a common theme you will hear is of regret for not having stayed more focused on, and not having more proactively stepped out toward, all that life has to offer. Legendary football coach Lou Holts offers good advice when he says, "If you are bored with life, if you don't get up every morning with a burning desire to do things, then you don't have enough goals."

University studies have shown that only three percent of the general population takes the time to write down specific goals. These studies have also shown that a very high percentage of people who *do* properly set goals eventually achieve those goals. This is an amazing finding.

In 1953, a study was conducted of graduating seniors at Yale University. Of that graduating class, only three percent had properly written goals; another ten percent had partially set goals; and eighty-seven had not taken the time to write down any goals for their life and career. Then, in 1973, some twenty years later, this study found that the three percent who had properly set goals had not only accomplished more than the other ninety-seven percent, but the study also revealed that the elite three percent was worth more financially than the entire other ninety-seven percent combined.

The late William Danforth, previously chairman of the board for Ralston Purina said, "I have observed that setting a goal makes no appeal to the mediocre. But to those fired with an ambition to really greatly achieve, setting a goal becomes a program that stirs the inner soul to action." Dr. Alexander Graham Bell adds, "What this power is I cannot say; all I know is that it exists and it becomes available only when a man is in that state of mind in which he knows exactly what he wants and is fully determined not to quit until he finds it." Business philosopher Jim Rohn writes, "The ultimate reason for setting goals is to entice you to become the person it takes to achieve them." He later adds, "The reason most people face the future with apprehension instead of anticipation is because they don't have it well designed."

The courageous life is one that embraces the responsibility to clearly define *what* one's life mission and dreams are, and *how* one is going to pursue those dreams while also growing in the other areas of life. Those living the courageous life are determined to own their lives and majestically sail toward their future and potential.

But if you set sail without clearly defined goals, you'll be like a ship without a rudder that can only drift aimlessly—always in danger of running ashore at some undetermined destination.

Understand that the ability to properly set goals, and then work toward their achievement, is what author and business consultant Brian Tracy calls the "master skill of success." He writes that "developing this skill will do more to ensure your success than anything else you could ever do. In twenty-five years of study and experience, I've come to the conclusion that success equals goals, and all else is commentary. Intense goal orientation is an essential characteristic of all high-achieving men and women. . . . It is not possible to realize even a fraction of your potential until you have learned how to set and achieve goals . . ."

Though this book is about pursuing your courageous dreams, you want to pursue your dreams while living a balanced and healthy life. You do not want to step out toward your dreams and leave your relationships and health behind. Thus, the pursuit of the courageous life will not only include defining your dreams, but it will also involve writing down specific goals for each dimension of life.

For example, while I have pursued my current dream of writing this book, I have carried with me a list of other goals for the various dimensions of my life. A sample of these goals is given below. Using this example, I now ask you to list the various dimensions of your life, and then create a list of specific goals for each area by asking the question, "What do I want to accomplish in this area of my life?"

1. My Personal Walk with God:

✳ Spend time with God in prayer and Bible reading six days a week (at least forty-five minutes)

✳ Read one spiritual book per month

✳ Serve in a leadership role in my church

2. My Role as a Husband & Father:

✳ Date Martha (my wife) two times each month, and my kids once a month

✳ Do two special things for Martha each month (card, flowers . . .)

✳ Take time to talk and catch up each day with each family member

✳ Say "thank you," encourage, and say "I love you" daily to each family member

✳ Take Martha on a weekend alone to Chicago by . . .

✳ Anniversary trip to Mexico in May

✳ Have one spiritual conversation with each child once a week

✳ Take boys to at least six University of Illinois sporting events each year

✳ Take the family to one Pro Baseball game each summer

✳ Take Austin & Calvin to the Indy 500 or NASCAR event

3. My Role as a Consultant:

✳ Make $/month in income by . . .

✳ Solicit three new contracts within . . .

✳ Contact each coaching client once a month outside regular meetings

✳ Contact one potential new client every week

✳ Finish first draft of book by . . .

4. My Social Life:

✳ Have lunch with at least two friends every month

✳ Call my mom, dad, and brothers at least once every two weeks

5. My Mental Life:

✳ Read one non-spiritual book per month

✳ Teach in a university setting twice a year (adjunct)

✳ Take a two-hour retreat once a week to think, prioritize, and plan

6. My Physical Life:

✳ Work out five days each week (four days on weights/five days cardio—minimum of forty-five minutes)

✳ Maintain weight at 195 pounds

7. My Financial Life:

❋ Give ten percent of income to ministry; save/invest ten percent of income

❋ Pay off Jeep by . . .

❋ Finish basement in . . .

❋ Buy big-screen TV by . . .

How to properly set goals

As you work on writing goals for each dimension of your life, the following three principles will help in that process.

As mentioned, the *first* principle is to understand that proper goal setting allows you to choose your own destiny in every area of life. Goals allow you to control the direction of your life by clearly defining what you want to achieve, and how you will continue to grow.

I remember my first real girlfriend in junior high. In a way, she was my dream girl. She was fun, witty, pretty, her older brothers were cool, and her family owned a swimming pool. She was everything a junior high boy would want. But I also remember that while I was "going out" with this girl, other areas of my life started to suffer from a lack of attention. For instance, I found myself spending more time with her and less time with my other friends. I also came to realize that having a girlfriend meant I was supposed to sit with her at every lunch, and sometimes even share my food with her.

As I learned all the rules of having a girlfriend in junior high, I began to feel overwhelmed. The list of obligations just got longer and longer. I had to visit at her locker in between classes, buy her a gift at Christmas, Valentine's Day, and on her birthday, and dance only with her at school dances! The most frustrating rule was the requirement to spend time almost every night talking with her on the phone, which took time away from my homework (which I did not care about) and television (which I did care about). Although I was spending time with a really nice girl, my life just seemed out of whack as a result. So after a few weeks of this, I asked her if we could "just be friends," and within just a few hours, I had my life back.

Just like that experience with my first girlfriend, if you're not careful, pursuing a dream can pressure you to neglect other areas of your life. And if you allow this neglect to go on for too long, a growing distaste for your courageous dream will likely take root and grow until you detest the very dream you want to live out. But carefully setting specific goals for *each* dimension of life will keep your dream from smothering your life. These goals will allow you to control how the pursuit of your dream will ultimately impact your life, and the lives of those around you.

The *second* principle to keep in mind is that your goals need to be *specific, measurable,* and *motivating.* Vague goals will always produce vague results. Therefore a goal should always answer two questions for you: (1) how much? and (2) by when? For example, "Read two books (*how much*) each month (*by when*)," "Lose ten pounds (*how much*) by June 30 (*by when*)," "Start saving ten percent of my income (*how much*) by increasing my saving donation by a half percent a month until I reach ten percent (*by when*)."

Yet as you know, there are always a few goals that you tend to consistently talk yourself out of. Even though you *want* to accomplish "such and such" a goal, for some reason you keep getting off track. For example, even though I may want to lose ten pounds by a certain date, I find progress hard to make because I really enjoy my wife's homemade chocolate chip cookies. And though I really want to lose those ten pounds, those cookies, and buckets of ice cream in our freezer, keep breaking down my resistance. I keep giving in to their enticing call to find a home in my stomach.

Well, for those goals that are a struggle to accomplish, an additional third question needs to be asked that will serve as an extra motivator. This third question is "Or what?"

For example: "Read two books (*how much*) each month (*by when*), or I will play no golf the following month (*or what*)"; "Lose ten pounds (*how much*) by June 30 (*by when*), or no trip to Cancun, Mexico, next spring (*or what*)"; "Start saving ten percent of my income by increasing my saving contributions by a half percent a month until I reach ten percent, or every month I don't make such an increase I will let my wife be in total control of the remote control when we watch TV." Motivators like these always help, especially since my wife prefers designer shows to Chicago Bears football.

Why do you sometimes need this third step to motivate you to accomplish goals you *want* to achieve? Why do you consistently talk yourself out of goals you honestly and deeply desire to carry out? Successful people understand it is a myth that an individual will automatically do what she believes is important, exciting, or easy. It's a myth that a person will naturally do what he wants to do. It does not matter how intelligent, strong, or spiritually mature you are, there will always be a few behaviors and actions that, even though you desire to do them, in your own strength you will not carry them out.

In one of his most authentic discourses in the Christian Bible, the Apostle Paul admits to this struggle in his own life. The struggle between doing what he wants to do versus doing what he knows is wrong. Paul wrote:

> "I don't understand myself at all, for I really want to do what it right, but I don't do it. Instead, I do the very thing I hate. . . . No matter which way I turn, I can't make myself do right. I want to, but I can't. When I want to do good, I don't. And when I try not to do wrong, I do it anyway. . . . It seems to be a fact of life that when I want to do what is right, I inevitably do what is wrong. For my inner being delights in God's law; but I see another law at work in the members of my body, waging war against the law of my mind and making me a prisoner to the law of sin at work in my members . . ."

In these personal thoughts, he admits his own frustration and struggle to conform his behaviors to his desires. And the same will be true for you and me, and this is why you need various forms of accountability in your life. The fact is, there will always be a few goals that you really want to achieve (to lose weight, save more money, etc.) that your lazy side will talk you out of. And you will keep losing this battle until you step up and add some accountability for your actions.

In my consulting practice I work with people in sales who are striving to increase their sales by using various methods, including setting goals. And although each salesperson I work with *wants* to achieve her goals, there are times when many months will go by before any progress is made, if at all. And when her progress is slow, this is when I have her answer that third question: "Or what?"

How a salesperson will answer this question is varied and often creative. For example, a person who is a staunch Republican may write out a check for $200 and give it to another person in the group with instructions to send it to the Democratic National Committee if his goal has not been accomplished by next month. Another idea we have used is that a pro-life salesperson will have to put a pro-choice sticker on his car for a month if he doesn't make his goal. These are two examples how answering the question "or what?" can be effectively used to motivate, and hold accountable, an individual who is struggling to reach a goal.

Whether it is giving your golf clubs to someone else to hold for a month if you do not reach a goal, or paying to have lunch brought in for the entire team, answers to the "or what?" question can be creative, but they always needs to be compelling—where the consequence and sting hurts *more* than not making progress on the goal.

If you *really* want to achieve a goal, if you're not just trying to make yourself feel good by having such-and-such written on your list of goals, then realize there will always be a few goals that you will need to add extra motivation. This will help you break through and accomplish those tasks that you *want* to do, yet for whatever reason are not completing.

In summary, as you create your list of goals for each dimension of life, remember your goals need to be specific, measurable, and motivating. *How much? By when? Or what?* Hopefully, most of your goals will only require answers to the first two questions, but rest assured, the third will be needed more than you would like!

The *final* principle to keep in mind is that your goals need to be aligned with your life-mission statement and personal strengths and values. When you sense that your goals are producing results that support your overall mission in life, you in turn will have greater incentive to perform more of those actions. Stephen Covey writes that we should always begin with the "end in mind," and the best way to do this is by making sure each of your goals is aligned with your life-mission statement, strengths, and values. And you accomplish this by asking the question, "Will this goal help me pursue my overall mission in life?"

If you look at my list of goals, each one helps me live out my life-mission statement, aligns with my values, and (if needed) uses my unique strengths. Some may do this more than others, but all my goals are common in this way. I mentioned earlier that I would like to play bass guitar in a traveling band. The reasons this wish is not one of my written goals is that (1) this desire does not align with my current strengths, (2) this lifestyle would not support my values at this point in life, and (3) this wish does not move me strategically forward in accomplishing my life mission.

But this could all change in the future . . . As I keep practicing, playing bass guitar could eventually become a strength of mine; when my kids are all away in college, I could then spend time playing with U2, Bruce Springsteen, Kenny Chesney, or Shania Twain (I am assuming a lot here) without compromising my values; and this could eventually support my mission to "reach my potential" as a world-class bass guitar player in a legendary band. So I still have hope!

But I am also honest enough to admit this should not be a focused goal of mine right now. Maybe down the road, but for now the other goals I am actively pursuing align much more closely with who I am, and where I want my life to go in the immediate future.

PUTTING YOUR ACTION PLAN TOGETHER

Abraham Lincoln said, "I will prepare and someday my chance will come." Well, all of your preparation work is now starting to crystallize and come together. Good job on taking the time to formulate your dreams, values, strengths, and goals!

A simple format for your action plan is given below. As you review this format, know that you have complete freedom to lay out your dreams and goals in any way that best fits your personality and learning style. The following format is only a suggested model. I know of people who have put their information on laminated three-by-five cards that they carry in their pocket. Others have written this information out on a large whiteboard in their office. One person tattooed her life dream and mission on her arm. The options are endless.

But I do recommend you start with the format given below, and then as you use this tool, revise it in ways that better fit your personality and learning style—like getting it tattooed on your arm so you can review it while riding your chopper!

Though the options for how it's done are endless, the need to create a plan is *not* optional, for a well-thought-through and written plan is critical to your success. Remember, "If you do not have a plan, you will probably work for someone who does." Your plan, however you construct it, will free you to live *your* life, pursue *your* dreams, and experience the exhilaration of reaching *your* ultimate potential.

You may be wondering, "Why do I need to put all this in *writing*? Why do I need to have a *written* copy of my goals and dreams?" Many leaders I work with say they have their goals stored in their memory, and thus they do not need to write them out.

Does this really work? Do we really need to write out our goals and dreams? Whenever a person tries to convince me that he doesn't need to put his goals in writing, I ask him this question: "How well are you presently doing in reaching your dreams and goals for each area of your life?" The answer is almost always, "not very well."

Yes, a person can have a vague idea in her mind of her goals and dreams, but this mental list will usually be short, somewhat foggy, and definitely not specific, measurable, and motivating.

Trust the experts. All the research in the science of success and goal-setting stresses the discipline of clarifying your goals in writing. What are you afraid of? I challenge you to stake your claim! Have the courage to write them out. I guarantee that if you do not complete the process described below, and do not make progress on the issues discussed in the next chapter, the probability that you will reach your potential will be significantly compromised.

Trust those who have gone before you. Choose to do the focused work of preparation so that when you finally take that courageous step out of your comfort zone, you will have everything you need to successfully live the courageous life. As Michelangelo quipped, "If people knew how hard I worked to get my mastery, it wouldn't seem so wonderful after all."

The recommended format to use for your action plan is as follows: Take the first draft of your life-mission statement, values, strengths, courageous dream, and the goals you have listed under each dimension of your life, and organize them on a computer word-processing document. The reason you want to input this on a computer document is so that you can easily revise your action plan and print off new copies when needed. Below is an example with some of my own information typed in.

You will notice that under the "courageous dream," you will need to spend time clarifying what your first five steps toward that dream will be. You can also keep a longer list of additional steps in your journal that can later be incorporated into the action plan after you accomplish the first five steps. You will need to continually update "My next five steps toward my dream" as you make progress toward your dream.

Life Purpose

"To Reach, and Mentor Others to Reach, Our Highest God-Given Potential, While Living a Balance Life."

Personal Values & Strengths

Core Values:

- Faith (intimacy with God)
- Family (intimacy with my family)
- Authentic relationships with others
- Reaching my full potential—being purpose-driven

- Life balance
- Freedom
- Self-discipline/self-control
- Being relevant

Strengths:

- Wisdom & discernment
- Systems thinking
- Focus (I focus well on tasks)
- Intentional relator (good at intentional relationships)

- Facilitating growth and learning
- Creative writing & teaching
- Listening

My Courageous Dream

To complete the first draft of my book on the courageous life by writing eight hours a week on this project.

My next five steps toward my dream:

1. Create an overall outline for the book by July 30

2. Create a specific outline for chapter one by August 15

3. Research chapter one by September 1

4. Write for a minimum of eight hours each week through September

5. Finish first draft of chapter one by September 30

Life Goals

1. My Personal Walk with God:

- Spend time with God in prayer and Bible reading six days a week (at least 45 minutes)
- Read one spiritual book per month
- Serve in a leadership role in my church

2. My Role as a Husband & Father:

- Date Martha (my wife) two times each month, and my kids once a month
- Do two special things for Martha each month (card, flowers . . .)
- Take time to talk and catch up each day with each family member
- Say "thank you," encourage, and say "I love you" daily to each family member
- Take Martha on a weekend alone to Chicago by . . .
- Anniversary trip to Mexico in May
- Have one spiritual conversation with each child once a week
- Take boys to at least six University of Illinois sporting events each year
- Take the family to one pro baseball game each summer
- Take Austin & Calvin to the Indy 500 or NASCAR event

3. My Role as a Consultant:

- Make $/month in income by . . .
- Solicit three new contracts within . . .
- Contact each coaching client once a month outside regular meetings
- Contact one potential new client every week
- Finish first draft of book by . . .

4. My Social Life:

- Have lunch with at least two friends every month
- Call my mom, dad, and brothers at least once every two weeks

5. My Mental Life:

- Read one non-spiritual book per month

- Teach in a university setting twice a year (adjunct)

- Take a two-hour retreat once a week to think, prioritize, and plan

6. My Physical Life:

- Work out five days each week (four days on weights/five days cardio—minimum of 45 minutes)

- Maintain weight at 195 pounds

7. My Financial Life:

- Give ten percent of income to ministry—save/invest ten percent of income

- Pay off Jeep by . . .

- Finish basement in . . .

- Buy big-screen TV by . . .

Congratulations! You have completed the first draft of the roadmap that will guide you on your epic journey. In the next chapter we'll discuss how to use your action plan each day from here on out. But as I close this chapter, I want to give a final thought as you ponder the document you have just created.

Remember, what you have completed is only a first draft. Spend the next few days, and weeks (however long it takes), to pray over, meditate on, and get feedback from a few others regarding what you have written. Take time to work with the words, make sure the goals align with your life mission, values, and strengths, and that the dream you have chosen from your list of options is the right one (i.e., you have chosen the dream that aligns the closest with your life mission, strengths, and values).

Digest what you have written, and when you feel you are ready to step outside your comfort zone, turn to the next chapter and start reading. If this does not happen, keep pondering and revising your plan until you start feeling the energy of new life, hope, and faith well up inside of you. Keep revising until you know you have it. Despite fears and doubts, your action plan represents what you honestly believe your life should stand for and accomplish.

Actor Jonathan Winters said, "If your ship does not come in, swim out to meet it!" Many people are waiting for their ship to come in. But I am asking you to join the few who refused to wait any longer and made the courageous choice to swim out to their ship. Don't wait any longer. Dive in! As we discussed at the beginning of this chapter, your *real job* awaits!

CHAPTER 7

A Dream Is Like a River...

A favorite song of mine is "Dream Weaver" by Gary Wright. The song was a hit on the radio back in 1976 when I was just entering high school and attempting to grow my first set of sideburns. They were more fuzz than true whiskers, but I was proud of them nevertheless.

Even to this day, whenever I hear that song, memories from my teen years rush into my mind, including playing football on Friday nights under dim stadium lights that cast more shadows than light on the football field. Other memories include learning how to drive on the back roads of rural Illinois and of having a crush on a cheerleader named Julie, who was one grade ahead of me in school. Since "Dream Weaver" is one of my all-time favorite songs, I tried to incorporate the lyrics into one of these chapters, but no matter how I try to manipulate its message, this song is more about escaping life than courageously pursuing your dreams. Oh, well.

But there is song by Garth Brooks called "The River" that expresses in a powerful and majestic way what the courageous life is all about. I heard the song a few years back when the head coach of my hometown's football team kept playing it over and over in the weight room. In a way, it became the team's theme song that year.

I highly recommend you purchase this song as a constant reminder, not only of your courageous choice to sail toward your dreams, but as a reminder that your journey will not always be easy. But you're not making the choice to pursue your dreams because it will be easy, you're choosing to pursue your courageous dreams because you must try. For if you do not attempt "to chance the rapids and dare to dance the tides," you won't only risk losing your dreams, you will experience deep disappointment and regret for having played it too safe in life.

BY YOURSELF, BUT NEVER ALONE

As the lyrics reflect, as you voyage down "the river" toward your dreams, in many ways your journey will be a lonely one. Many times you will need to travel the river and pass through the torrential white-waters and rapids alone. This is because many of the fears, doubts, and barriers that you will need to overcome reside within yourself and are very personal in nature. They are unique to who you are and to the dream you are pursuing.

I remember taking my driver's license test after turning sixteen. It was so exciting to finally be able to get my license and be free to travel the many highways and byways of central Illinois. But before receiving my driver's license, I had to overcome a few fears and barriers—namely the driver's exam, which had to be taken with an old instructor who looked like Santa Claus, but with the social skills of the Grinch.

I remember walking out to my car for the driving portion of the exam. I was alone. I had no family or friends to protect me from the old Santa Grinch who was walking only a few feet behind me. But the dream to get my license pressed me onward, so I got into the car with that old instructor, and drove away. The driving exam was going well until the Santa Grinch told me to turn the wrong way down a one-way street, which I proceeded to do. After realizing what happened, I knew I was doomed. Needless to say, I did not pass the driving exam that day.

As you travel the river toward your dreams, there will be stretches of the river you must travel alone—where alone you must face the obstacles and fears that lie just under the water. This is a reality of the courageous journey.

But be encouraged! Even though there will be times you must navigate the river solo, your trip does not need to be traveled in complete solitude. There will be opportunities along the way where friends can encourage and help propel you forward by providing help, wisdom, and encouragement. Just as I had family and friends help me prepare (and then re-prepare) to succeed in getting my driver's license, so others will play a critical role in helping you reach your dreams as well.

YOUR POWER TO CHOOSE

This chapter will focus your attention on two important issues. The first will be how to successfully use the action plan created in the last chapter. The second will be how to construct a compelling environment around you that will help propel you toward your dreams, no matter what fear or obstacle is faced along the way. But as we prepare to discuss these two issues, there is one underlying choice that permeates them both—an ongoing choice that will play a central role in determining whether you successfully reach your dreams and goals.

This choice is the decision to take action. To set out each day and take the specific steps needed to move toward your dream. Where every day you do what is needed to effectively use your action plan *and* create an environment that will move you forward in the courageous life.

The pursuit of a dream always starts with believing in who we are, and having faith in what we want to become. But your faith must also be accompanied with action. Positive thoughts without specific action will always achieve nothing. This chapter is founded on the central truth that in order to reach a dream, you will need to decide to be a person of action, who seizes the moment by courageously choosing to move toward that dream each day. And this choice to act will not always be an easy one.

As you have worked through the processes of clarifying your fears, self-talk, values, strengths, life mission, dreams and goals, you may have thought, "If I choose to pursue a dream, it will take a lot of focus and hard work!" You're right. The courageous life is not easy and your dreams are not something you can just wish into existence. The journey down the river will not always be easy, and there is a price you must be willing to pay.

I like getting things for free. Though I desire to live by the creed "to give is better than to receive," in all honesty my motives are not always this pure. While I know this to be true about myself, I do realize that my dreams and goals will never be given to me for free. They will take hard work and sacrifice. For instance, this book I am writing has taken concerted time and effort to complete. I have had to remain focused and carefully choose how to spend my time each week so that time (and energy) could be freed up to write, write, write, and write. I have had to pay a price to pursue this dream of mine, and so will you.

A college professor gave a test to seniors who would soon be graduating and entering the workforce. The test was divided into three separate categories and the students were free to choose from any one of the three sections. The first category of questions was the hardest and worth fifty points. The second was easier and worth forty points. The third, the simplest, was worth thirty points. Upon completion of the test, *all* of the students who had chosen to answer the hardest fifty point questions were given As for just attempting to complete the questions. Students who chose the forty-point questions were all given Bs, and those who attempted the easiest questions received Cs. As you might suspect, some of the students were frustrated by such a grading scale and asked the professor why he graded the test this way. The professor leaned over the podium, smiled and said, "I wasn't testing your knowledge. I was testing your ambitions."

Many people want to take the easy way in life—to take the path of least resistance where they set their goals so low that accomplishing them requires little effort and sacrifice. Deep down they expect nothing of real consequence to happen . . . so nothing ever does. But the courageous life is not easy, and your dreams will never be given to you for free. You will need to make deliberate choices to walk away from the television, Internet, junk food, or whatever else entices you, and make the sacrifices necessary to reach the summit of your dreams.

Your life is the sum total of the choices you have made so far. Where you are currently spiritually, economically, socially, and physically is a result of the choices made since the time you were young. My challenge is to choose wisely from here on out. The good news is that your future choices can lead you through invigorating experiences of renewal and growth. Trust me and those who have gone before you in this courageous quest: the sacrifice and hard work will be *more* than worth it! The courageous life will leave you with no regrets.

How to successfully use your action plan

We will now discuss how to use the action plan created in the previous chapter. Good job in taking the time to create this plan! As you finish revising the plan, the three guidelines provided below will enable you to use it effectively.

The first guideline is to review your action plan every day. Specifically, take a few minutes to do three things: (1) read your goals, (2) visualize mental pictures of your goals already accomplished, and (3) cultivate thoughts of belief that your goals are indeed attainable.

When doubts start to cloud your mind, it will be this daily habit of reviewing your dreams and goals, and *choosing* to think thoughts of belief, that will enable you to keep moving forward, no matter what fears and doubts arise within you. "Everything is possible for him who believes," and it will be the discipline of reviewing your goals each day that will help train your thinking to maintain a perspective of belief regarding your future. Claude Bristol (who worked for the *Stars and Stripes* newspaper during World War I in addition to being a best-selling author) wrote, "I would like to point out that hard work alone will not bring success. The world is filled with people who have worked hard but have little to show for it. Something more than hard work is necessary; it is creative thinking and firm belief in your ability to execute your ideas. The successful people in history have succeeded through their thinking. Their hands were merely helpers of their brains."

Carry your action plan wherever you go. Put a copy near your computer at work and at home. Keep a copy in your daily planner, and even a reduced laminated copy in your pocket. There will be plenty of times when you have some extra time, or are sitting through a meeting where the speaker is just rambling, when you can get out your action plan and spend time reviewing and visualizing. I personally like to keep a smaller version of my action plan handy so it can be studied when I have some extra time waiting for a person to show up for a meeting, or when listening to some long-winded presenter. But the point is to review, visualize, and turn your thoughts toward belief every day, all through the day.

In *The Success Principles*, Jack Canfield shares that when Olympic decathlon gold medalist Bruce Jenner asked a roomful of Olympic hopefuls if they had a written list of goals, everyone raised their hands. When he asked how many had their list with them at that moment, only one person raised his hand. That person was Dan O'Brien. And it was Dan O'Brien who went on to win the gold medal in the decathlon at the 1996 Olympics in Atlanta.

Don't underestimate the power of setting goals and reviewing them every day. Reviewing your action plan each day will cement your dreams and goals into your mind and embolden you to take steps away from your comfort zone toward those dreams—whether the dream is an Olympic medal, starting a business, becoming physically fit, or any other vision pounding deep within your heart.

Second, use your action plan to actively program your subconscious mind by taking *extended* time for focused visualization. As just mentioned, when reviewing your action plan throughout the day, you can create sudden images in the mind that portray your dreams and goals being realized. But in addition, a second habit you need to develop is to take *extended* time to visualize the accomplishment of your dreams, thereby helping to significantly accelerate their achievement.

While your subconscious mind will move into action once it starts to receive your goals through the habit of reviewing them throughout the day, your subconscious mind will move much more powerfully and quickly when your dreams and goals are accompanied by mental "pictures" of the final desired outcomes. Though these mental pictures may be faint or sketchy, they will be sufficient for the subconscious to act upon.

Research has found that the brain goes through the same processes whether an activity is visualized or actually done by the body. A study at Harvard University found that people who visualized in advance a specific task performed that task with nearly one hundred percent accuracy, whereas people who did not visualize the task achieved only fifty-five percent accuracy. Visualization is one of the most powerful yet underutilized tools of success you can incorporate into your life.

Visualization activates the creative powers of the subconscious mind in ways that will makes a person much more aware of opportunities that can help her achieve her dreams and goals. When you continually impress vivid pictures of a goal into the subconscious, it will immediately seek to create ways to accomplish that goal.

Haven't you experienced times when you've tried to figure out a solution to a problem, but couldn't come up with an answer? Then later that day, or week, the solution fires into your conscious thought, seemingly from out of nowhere! This is the power of your subconscious mind working to find a solution to the problem, even when your *conscious* mind had long moved on to something else.

I am always amazed when this happens, and am reminded this is an awesome gift that needs to be used in a proactive way.

Once you start to program your subconscious mind by focused visualization, be very alert to the hunches and ideas that come to you from that moment forward. Many people throw their genius and creative ideas in the garbage because they think an idea is stupid or impossible, or because they received unenthusiastic feedback about the idea from a friend or relative.

As a consultant, when I work with clients who are struggling to uncover a solution to a specific problem, I challenge them to find the best solution by simply impressing into their subconscious mind a picture of the preferred outcome, in addition to any facts that may be relevant to the problem.

I then tell them to trust their subconscious mind to work on the solution for them. In my years of using this technique, I have found it never fails to produce a solution, as long as the person is disciplined in driving the issue into their mind on a regular basis.

For instance, there was a client who just could not find time to accomplish his goal to run and lift weights four times each week. He complained of being too busy during the day and too tired in the evenings—and whenever he did start to work out, he would eventually drift out of the habit. I challenged him to vividly imprint a picture into his mind, a picture of himself running, lifting weights, and feeling good about it. I added that he had to do it each day, and continue for the next few weeks.

I also instructed him to provide his mind with the facts of his schedule and fatigue in the evenings. I told him not to force a solution, but if he was patient, the right solution would eventually come into his mind . . . And two weeks later, it did! While relaxing on a flight home from a business trip, the solution suddenly came to him in a bold flash. The solution was simple, but one he had never thought of before. With an adjustment in his morning routine, one that he'd previously believed was impossible to change, he freed up time to visit the gym four mornings each week. He also wrapped some additional accountability around his plan by agreeing to pick up a friend on his way to the gym each morning.

When you take *extended* time to visualize pictures of your completed dreams and goals, you will start to make unexpected movement toward their accomplishment. All of a sudden, new ideas will pop into your mind; you will see opportunities you never noticed before; you will be emboldened to ask someone for help or advice; and/or you will begin to see creative ways to bring your dreams into reality. Movement will happen!

The process of extended visualization is a simple one. All you need to do is relax your body and mind, close your eyes, and see your dreams and goals as already complete. Take ten to fifteen minutes each day to clearly and emotionally picture your dream and goals in your mind. Do not concern yourself with how your dreams will be accomplished. Just leave that to your subconscious mind, which has its own way of making contacts and opening doors that you never thought of. And when an idea flows into your mind, follow it with faith. Keep a pad and pencil near so these ideas will never be lost—and then by faith act upon them. This is one way the courageous life becomes very exciting and fun!

Take time each day to (1) review your dreams and goals, and (2) see and feel their accomplishment in the privacy of your own mind and thoughts. Visualization is one of the most powerful tools of success, so make sure you use this tool by taking a few minutes each day to develop the habit.

The *final* choice surrounding your action plan involves the one dream you have elected to pursue. My challenge to you is to commit to take *one* step toward your "courageous dream" every day, five days a week. If you went into the woods each day and took just one swing at a large oak tree with a sharp ax, one day that great oak tree would fall to the ground. In the same way, if you take one swing at your dream each day, one day it will fall into your life, for as one of America's original authors on the topic of success, Robert Collier writes, "Success is the sum of small efforts, repeated day in and day out."

I have two special memories of when my family was stationed at an air force base in Alabama during my fifth-grade year in school. One memory is of holding hands with a girl named Jennifer, and the second is of walking around vacant fields near my home looking for empty soda bottles. Each glass bottle was worth a nickel, and when enough were found, I would run to the drugstore and turn in the bottles for the refund money—which was then given right back to the cashier to pay for a handful of candy!

I recall walking through vacant fields for hours in the heat and humidity scrounging for all kinds of bottles, and how my heart started to pound when I saw the glitter of glass under some bush or pile of garbage. I kept adding up the money until there was enough to purchase my candy for the day, as the lure of those sugar-filled Pixy Stix, jawbreakers, and gumballs kept me focused and determined to find bottles . . . one at a time.

One of the best ways to stay focused on making daily progress on your goals and dreams is to track your progress. Just as I kept close track of the number of bottles collected, successful organizations and people keep accurate track of the progress they are making toward their mission and goals by taking time to accurately assess where they have been and how much farther they still have to go.

Tracking one's progress is very natural. I remember as a child trying to hold my breath for thirty seconds, then forty-five seconds, then for one minute, then two minutes (though I admit after about sixty seconds I would fake it by quietly breathing through my nose while keeping my lips tightly shut and cheeks puffed out). As a football player in high school, I kept track of the number of tackles made while playing defensive end; and during basketball, kept similar records of my scoring, rebounding, and turnovers. I always knew that if the numbers were not changing for the better, I was not changing for the better!

Successful leaders keep track of what they want more of. Vinod Khosla, the founding CEO of Sun Microsystems, said, "It's great to know how to recharge your batteries. But it's even more important to make sure you actually do it. I track how many times I get home in time to have dinner with my family; my assistant reports the exact number to me each month . . . My goal is to be home for dinner at least twenty-five nights a month. Having a target number is key. I know of people in my business who are lucky if they make it home five nights a month. I don't think that I'm any less productive than those people." Now that you have decided what you want in life, and have it written in your action plan, you need to keep record of the progress. On the following page is a courageous growth chart that can be used to track the progress toward your goals and dreams. (You can print this out each month on the backside of your action plan.)

On the courageous growth chart, track your progress on all, or a selection of your goals, while *also* charting your daily steps toward your courageous dream. As you track your progress, you will then have a monthly record of how well you are growing in the various areas of your life. The key is to make progress, and then to record that progress as a reminder of where you have been and where you are going. This chart will also provide excellent feedback for your life. There have been times when I thought I was exercising regularly when my courageous growth chart revealed that this was indeed not the case.

My challenge is that, in addition to working on your goals, you take at least five steps every week toward your courageous dream. These steps may be large or small, but some type of progress must be made. For example, if your dream is to participate in an iron-man triathlon, then one day your step toward your dream may be to research training programs on the Internet, the second day you may do more research, the third day you may find information regarding various races, the fourth day you may buy running shoes, the fifth day you may research the type of bicycle you will need . . .

After you have all the information, your five steps toward your dream each week may simply be to work out five days a week using the workout plan you created. Then, as you get closer to the race, you will need to accomplish other tasks, which include packing and preparing your equipment for the race. But step by step, taking at least five steps every week, you will get there. The tracking chart will be your proof. Proof that you are taking initiative and living the courageous life!

MONKEY SEE, MONKEY DO

Good job! I congratulate you for taking the initiative to use your action plan and create your courageous growth chart. These tools will provide an effective roadmap as you step out to live the courageous life. I applaud your effort, which now places you in the top three percent alongside those who have taken the time to clarify in writing what they want to achieve in their life.

Now, as you spend time reviewing, visualizing, and taking action steps toward your goals and dreams, you will soon begin to see progress. You will also experience the exhilaration of knowing you are on a path that's leading toward your potential. There are few better feelings in this life. Leadership expert John Maxwell writes, "Growth is happiness. Show me a person who is growing and they are happy. Show me a person who has leveled off and they only focus on yesterday."

We'll conclude this chapter by discussing an issue that will greatly influence the *rate* at which you attain your dreams and goals. This issue has to deal with your environment. Those who are highly successful in life are careful to create a supportive environment around them. They understand that the environment surrounding them will play a critical role in how efficiently and effectively they reach their potential.

(SAMPLE): Courageous Growth!

Charting Progress for: _____ (month, year)

Courageous dream: Make progress toward my dream at least five days a week (*see action plan for next five steps*).

	1	2	3	4	5	**6**	**7**	8	9	10	11	12	**13**	**14**	15	16
Write Book						■	■						■	■		

	17	18	19	**20**	**21**	22	23	24	25	26	**27**	**28**	29	30	31
Write Book				■	■						■	■			

	1	2	3	4	5	6	7	8	9	10	11	12	13	14	15	16	17	18	19	20	21	22	23	24	25	26	27	28	29	30	31
Pray 6 days/week																															
Read Bible 6 days/week																															
Review goals 1/day																															
Drink 2 glasses of H2O/day																															
Tell family "I Love You"																															
Encourage family daily																															
Exercise 4/week																															
Verbalize/visualize goals																															
1 on 1 extended conversation with Martha																															
Date Martha 2/month																															
Special thing for Martha 2/month																															
Take each child out for meal each month																															
Spiritual conversation with each child 1/week																															
Call parents & brothers 2/month																															
2 lunches/month w/friends																															
Read 1 Spiritual book/month																															
Read 2 other books/month																															
2 hours/week to think/plan																															

Looking back on my life, many of my best and worst behaviors were directly influenced by the environment in which I chose to imbed myself. One night during my senior year in high school, five of my friends and I went into a grocery store and bought eggs and rolls of toilet paper. It doesn't take a rocket scientist to know we were up to no good. If six high school boys walk into a store on Halloween night to buy eggs, toilet paper (and candy), then mischief is in the air.

Our plan was to get back at a girl who had put shaving cream on my friend's car earlier in the week. I distinctly remember that night knowing what I was about to do was wrong. Teepeeing was no big deal, but I knew that throwing raw eggs at a house was going too far; however, my friends and I were on a roll. Despite my hesitancy, I proceeded to sit in the bed of my friend's pickup truck as he drove to the girl's neighborhood, where we then teepee'd and unloaded multiple cartons of eggs onto her house—until her father came out the front door with a shotgun. Though that night provided me with one of the best adrenaline rushes ever, to this day I regret throwing those eggs. And though I chose my conduct that evening, that choice was greatly influenced by the people with whom I'd associated that night.

On the other hand, in college I would periodically give my sack lunch to a homeless person seen regularly near the college campus. Even though there were times I questioned whether giving away my lunch was necessary, I would go ahead and give him my lunch bag filled with a sandwich and assortment of other food. I was prompted to do this by an article that told of a businessman who would often give his lunch to homeless people while commuting to work in downtown New York City.

Though you ultimately choose your actions, your choices are greatly *influenced* by the environment that surrounds you, including the people with whom you associate and the things you see and read.

In fact, self-made millionaire Jim Rohn has said, "You are the average of the five people you spend the most time with." You are the average of those five people financially, spiritually, emotionally, and socially. Just as your behavior is influenced by changes in temperature or noises around you, so your behavior will be affected by the books you read, the people with whom you associate, the spouse you choose to marry, the pictures you hang in your office, the quotes you place on your desk, the food you choose to keep in the kitchen, the church, synagogue, or other religious organization you choose to attend (or not), the neighborhood in which you live, and the television shows you choose to watch. Each of these will project their influence (for good or for bad) into your life.

Brian Tracy writes, "Unfortunately, unless you control them carefully, most of the suggestions in your environment will tend to be negative. The radio, television, and newspapers are full of 'negative sensationalism.' Most of the conversations are filled with carping, complaining, and condemning . . . The key to your mental programming is for you to take systematic and purposeful control of your suggestive environment. It is for you to create a mental world that is predominantly positive and consistent with the person you want to be and the life you want to live."

Here are *four* ways to control your "suggestive environment":

1 You become like the people with whom you associate

The *first* way to manage your environment is to carefully select the people with whom you associate. The truth is you do not *have* to hang around with just anybody. Most of the time you do have the power to choose, and therefore you need to make the choice to spend time with people who are happy, positive, fun, kind, considerate, and who are growing in their life and reaching their own potential. Since you become like the people with whom you associate, it is critically important that you proactively spend time with individuals you want to be like. Mark Twain writes, "keep away from people who belittle your ambitions. Small people always do that, but the really great, make you feel that you too can become great."

Are there people in your life who tend to be negative, complain, and who blame others for the circumstances in their life? Are there individuals who judgmental, spread their negative trash around, and persist in projecting a victim mentality? If so, stop spending time with them! These people will erode your confidence and leave you feeling that your dreams and goals are unrealistic and not worth fighting for. If allowed, they will lead you directly back into the mediocre life.

Though there will always be some negative and de-energizing people with whom you have to work or live, you do need to insulate yourself as much as possible from the effects of their critical and negative thinking, beliefs, and behaviors. You can do this by not only limiting your contact with them, but by proactively infusing positive, constructive, and faith-filled words into your conversations with them. For example, when I find myself in a conversation where the dialogue is starting to become critical of a person who is not present, I try to infuse a few positive and supportive comments regarding that person. Most of the time this helps to turn the conversation in a more positive and optimistic direction.

While taking control of the negative influences around you, you also need to intentionally spend time with individuals who believe in you and motivate you to reach out toward your potential. Since you become like the people with whom you associate, you must proactively spend time with individuals who are successful, positive, spiritually centered, and who are stepping away from their own comfort zones to pursue their dreams. This special group of people will play a critical role in helping you stay focused and faithful to the courageous life. Albert Schweitzer writes, "In everyone's life, at some time, your inner fire goes out. It is then burst into flame by an encounter with another human being. We should all be thankful for those people who rekindle the inner spirit." John Maxwell writes, "Many people go far in life because someone else thought they could."

There are specific people with whom I purposely try to spend time—individuals who keep the flame in my heart burning by strengthening my belief in myself and by providing wise counsel regarding how to succeed. These mentors are living the courageous life and are happy to assist me as well. And in most cases, their wisdom, knowledge, and experience can be attained merely for the price of lunch or breakfast, when I invite them out for a meal, prepared to ask questions and then to listen.

There has never been a person who reached his dreams alone. No matter what success an individual accomplishes in life, somebody was there to help that person along the way.

Make a conscious effort to spend time with positive, supportive, and faith-filled people who believe in you, your dreams, and who are willing to help you live the courageous life. And make sure you always show appreciation for their time, encouragement, and relationships—for your appreciation will be the currency with which you pay them for their help and support.

John Wooden, one of the greatest coaches in history, taught his basketball players at UCLA that if a fellow player passed them the ball because they were in a better position to score, the one who did the scoring should always nod to, and thank, the one who had passed him the ball. One day a player said to Wooden, "Suppose he's not looking?" Coach Wooden simply said, "He'll be looking."

Whenever you receive encouragement and help from your special team of mentors, always take the time to acknowledge what they have done to help you score! Everyone needs words of encouragement and appreciation, and the words "thank you" and "I appreciate you" will be all the payment most of these friends and mentors will ever need.

2 Form a courageous society

A second way to intentionally create an environment for success is to form what I call a "courageous society." A courageous society is a small group of like-minded individuals who meet on a monthly basis to hold each other accountable to living the courageous life. This group of three to seven individuals will all have gone through the process of clarifying their life-mission statement, goals, and dreams—and have also embraced the fact that they will never be able to reach these objectives alone. They have acknowledged their need for the help, encouragement, and accountability of a close group of friends and peers.

You will definitely need the help of others in your quest. One of the wisest leaders of all time, King Solomon, wrote, "Two are better than one, because they have a good return for their work: If one falls down, his friend can help him up. But pity the man who falls and has no one to help him up! Also, if two lie down together, they will keep warm. But how can one keep warm alone? Though one may be over-powered, two can defend themselves. A cord of three strands is not quickly broken."

The purpose of a courageous society is to encourage, guide, and hold each person in the group accountable to make ongoing progress in the courageous life. This will be a close-knit group of friends who believe in each other and in the dream each member is pursuing.

The format for each monthly meeting is simple. After a time of greetings, one person takes five to ten minutes to share with the entire group a challenge from a book they read, or another growth idea recently learned. The person who provides this challenge is rotated among the group members, with one person sharing each month. After this time of learning, the remaining time is divided equally, where one by one, each person shares what he has specifically done over the past month to move toward the accomplishment of his coura-geous dream. While he may mention the progress he is making on his other goals, the focus is on the dream he is currently pursuing.

During this time the other group members remain quiet and lis-ten to what the individual is saying. Group members are listening for marked progress, fears, excuses, defensive comments, a victim mentality, requests for wisdom or guidance, and other pertinent issues. After the person has finished sharing what he has specifically accomplished over the past month to move toward his dream, the other group members then provide feedback, helpful suggestions, and encouragement.

While this feedback is being given, the person who just shared remains quiet and can only ask clarifying questions. No defensive comments or excuses are allowed. Only clarifying questions, and the words, "thank you for your thoughts and feedback" are permitted.

During this time, each group member embraces his need for feedback and the fact that this "truth will set him free." It will be in the context of this safe and honest group of friends that one will gain the wisdom needed to succeed in the courageous life.

The goal is to help each person fight through fears, perceived barriers, lack of knowledge, or whatever else is hindering their progress. This is not meant to be a feel-good meeting where everyone just pats each other on the back and sings "Kumbaya." This is to be a society of like-minded individuals who want the honest support and guidance from a closely knit group of individuals who have embraced the courageous life. Before the group moves on to the next person, the individual who is sharing will determine and verbally commit to the group the action step(s) they will make toward their dream in the next month. These are recorded and then reviewed by the individual at the next monthly meeting.

Rest assured, there will be times when additional forms of accountability will be needed to help an individual in the group make progress toward their dream. This accountability can look much like what was described in the last chapter regarding the "or what?" question. There will be times when certain fears, excuses, and barriers cause a person in the group to stagnate. This is when answering the "or what?" question will be beneficial. For example, a group member will commit to make "such-and-such" progress toward her dream, or else she'll give each person in the group twenty dollars, shave her head, take the group golfing, or another motivating idea.

Each individual in the courageous society should leave the meeting feeling encouraged, challenged, and with a clear understanding of what his next steps are. Though there will be times when constructive feedback is given, the meetings should always be energizing, positive, focused, supportive, with each member encouraged to continue sailing toward his dream.

Monthly meetings are to be a high priority for each group member, with individuals allowed to miss only two times each year. (The group can decide this number.)

3 Fill your world with icons

A third way to create an environment to help propel you toward a dream is to fill your surroundings with various "icons" that represent and remind you of that dream. An icon is an image, picture, or likeness that stands for and represents a certain object or idea. For example, in the Eastern Orthodox Church, the icon is generally a flat panel painting depicting a holy being or object such as Christ, Mary, saints, angels, or the cross. A religious icon may also be cast in metal, carved in stone, embroidered on cloth, done in mosaic work, or printed on paper or metal.

Icons serve the purpose of reminding us of that which is most important. As you pursue your dream, you can put pictures that represent your dream in your pocket, home, and office. You can also place quotes on walls and use symbolic objects that help keep you inspired and focused on the dream you have chosen to pursue.

A powerful example of how a simple icon can inspire an individual, or an entire team of individuals, is a wooden sign mounted on the brick wall outside the locker room of Notre Dame's football team. The sign reads, "Play Like A Champion Today." The slogan "play like a champion today" is so synonymous with the university that the rumor is Father Edward Sorin, the school's founder, received this quote as divine revelation back in 1842. While the exact origin of the slogan is not known, a tradition has developed over the years where each football player will hit the sign as they leave the locker room to make their way onto the football field for a game.

Former player Ryan Harris said of that sign, "(Whenever I see it) I think 'Why not? Why not today? Why not this game? Why not right now?' You came to Notre Dame to be a champion and every time I see it, I think 'Why not? Let's go do it!'" Another player, Carlyle Holiday recalls, "The guys take it seriously, so it meant a lot to me. I knew you had to come out with intensity when you hit that sign." Former Coach Lou Holts adds, "Regardless of the won-loss record, regardless of the problems you have, when you walk out on that field you have an obligation to your teammates and the fans to play to the best of your ability—to play like a champion and to think like a champion. But, I also asked my players that every time they hit that sign, to think about all the sacrifices your family has made; your teammates made in high school; the sacrifices your teachers have made; and you also think of the thousands of people who would love to be in your position. Just think about how fortunate we are. All of these thoughts should go through your mind when you hit that sign—*'Play Like A Champion Today.'*"

That old wooden sign outside Notre Dame's locker room has inspired many football players through the years to play at their highest level when they walked onto their football field. And we can place similar types of icons in our home, office, wallet, bathroom mirror, or wherever, to remind us of our potential, and the need to remain faithful to the dream we have chosen to pursue.

4 Take time to think courageously

The final piece of your environment you need to shape carefully is your weekly calendar. This is where you are vigilant in scheduling time away on a weekly basis to review your action plan, think through the progress you have made, and determine what needs to be done next. The pace of our society does not encourage reflective thinking, but it will be during these times alone that your knowledge will be transformed into wisdom—where you can process the experiences of the past week and put them into perspective; and where emerging ideas can be nurtured, refined, and put into action.

John Maxwell said, "Reflective thinking enables you to distance yourself from the intense emotions of particularly good or bad experiences and see them with fresh eyes. You can see the thrills of the past in the light of emotional maturity and examine tragedies in the light of truth and logic." Socrates observed, "The unexamined life is not worth living."

Set aside at least one and a half hours each week where you get away by yourself, with no distractions, and evaluate your life. It will be during these times that you can record thoughts in your personal journal, assess the past week in light of your dreams and goals, and make proactive plans for the future.

People who develop this habit may give up one or two hours a week to think and plan, but they will gain four to eight hours the following week as a result of living and working more efficiently. This is because when an individual takes the time to assess and learn from the past week, and then wisely plan their next week, they move through their lives proactively instead of reactively. They are prepared to lead themselves, versus being led by the expectations and "wants" of others. Yet the sad fact is, though the benefits of reflective thinking are proven and true, most people spend more time planning their summer vacations than they do planning their lives. Don't make this mistake! David Schwartz writes, "Where success is concerned, people are not measured in inches, or pounds, or college degrees, or family background; they are measured by the size of their thinking." Take time each week to think well. Take time to think big!

In this chapter we have considered two core issues. The first is how to use your action plan, and the second is how to shape your environment to help propel you forward in the courageous life. Implementing these steps will enable you to wisely and effectively maneuver the river leading to your dreams.

Believe in yourself. Your dreams are in sight! With the help of your action plan and close friends, look forward to the exhilaration you will feel when you reach the summit of your dream!

In the closing two chapters we will discuss some final thoughts regarding the courageous life, but before we do, I want to briefly address a particular matter that may affect some couples.

The support of your spouse

When two people become a couple, their lives, future, hopes, and dreams become intimately interwoven. Yet occasionally when a spouse enters into this courageous process, the other partner will become fearful when they see their spouse starting to pursue a dream. The reason for these fears may be similar to the causes discussed in an earlier chapter, but what should a person do when their spouse is not enthusiastic about the dream they want to pursue?

First, I have found that if both partners are encouraging *each other* to go through this process of clarifying and pursuing each of their own dreams, many of these issues will start to fade away. As each encourages and helps to enable the other's dream, then both will be experiencing the same feelings of excitement about the future. If only one person is engaged in this process, then many times the other will feel left out and fearful where it may all lead.

Second, some partners may initially experience feelings of fear when they hear about the other person's dream, but when given ample time to process and have a dialogue about what pursuing the dream will actually mean to their relationship and family, these fears slowly start to subside. The initial doubts and worries begin to dissipate because the couple has taken time together to process the ramifications of pursuing the courageous life.

Making a mutual decision to pursue the courageous life is critically important to the peace and harmony of a relationship. Thus if a mutual decision cannot be attained for some reason, this is a sign to stop and evaluate the dream, and other issues in your marriage, in more detail before moving forward.

Finally, if your spouse simply refuses to support your dream, then this may be a sign of one of two things. First it may be a sign that the plan you have created to pursue your dream is truly flawed in some way. I would recommend you discuss the specifics of your plan with some trusted advisors to get their input, involving your partner in these dialogues so they can hear firsthand what is on your mind and what changes will be made regarding how the dream will be pursued. The second sign might be there are some significant and deeper issues, or hurts from the past, in your relationship that have not been properly healed or dealt with. Your partner may not be rejecting your dream so much as they are frustrated with your relationship. The discussions regarding your dream are just surfacing deeper issues in your marriage that need to be addressed first.

I have found that there is no better support than my spouse in the courageous life. My wife is my biggest fan and champion, and while I have had to go through many of these steps with her, if they are wisely followed, your dream can (in time) obtain the encouragement of your partner. Be patient, move wisely, and give ample time for your dream to gain the support of your cherished spouse so that when the day comes when your dream is finally realized, they will be the one sending up the biggest cheer!

CHAPTER 8

Believe in What
You Do Not See

It's always inspiring to hear about individuals who have made the courageous choice to step through fears and overcome formidable barriers to pursue a dream. Michael Stadther is someone who did just that. Ever since he was a child growing up in Alabama, Michael had been intrigued with treasure hunts, and so later in life he conceived what others called his "impossible dream." His dream was to write a book that would contain clues to a real-life treasure hunt, leading to jewels worth a total of one million dollars. So one day he sat down and started to write a book for children and adults titled *A Treasure's Trove: A Fairy Tale about Real Treasure for Parents and Children of All Ages.*

The book led readers to twelve tokens hidden in public places scattered across the United States of America, and all one needed to do to find any of the diamonds, rubies, and a rare Kashmir sapphire, was to decipher the clues contained within the story of his book. The clues led to twelve tokens hidden across the country, which could then be redeemed for the jewel each token represented.

But Michael's dream was not easily realized. After sharing his book with every major publisher, he could not convince any of them on the merits of his treasure hunt. Every publisher turned him down. With the odds stacked against him, he regrouped and decided to publish the book himself. Michael was a first-time author with no publisher, no marketing, no distribution system, and no contracts with the bookstore chains. Yet he refused to give up.

As mentioned, *A Treasure's Trove* was the realization of Michael's twenty-five-year-old vision to create a real-life treasure hunt, with clues sandwiched between the pages of a fairy tale. He was initially inspired by a book published in 1979, titled *Masquerade,* which gave clues to a hidden necklace made of rare gems and gold that was eventually found by a reader in the English countryside three years later. As a teen he had read this book and dreamed that one day, he too would write such a real-life treasure hunt book.

Michael wanted his adventure to attract treasure hunters of all ages, while also developing the problem-solving, comprehension, and exploring skills of the reader. And though Michael understood *what* he wanted to do, it took him eight years to figure out *how* to do it. And while he never intended to go through the rigors of self-publishing his book, he now says that all the publishers who rejected his book, some rather unkindly, did him a huge favor. For by doing it himself—from the writing and illustrating (each picture took about three hundred hours), to learning Adobe Photoshop and buying the rights to the photographs featured in the puzzle workbook—Michael not only had creative control of his book, he also made a lot more money.

The initial two-million-dollar investment for his dream came from a software company he had sold a few years before, with his biggest expenditure being the crafting of twelve jewels, which were all based on various forest creatures. Michael also decided to hire his own marketing firm to create a website to promote and provide information on the book and its release. They also did something that isn't common in the book publishing industry; they purchased sixty-second radio spots targeting twelve major markets in the United States. They also paid for one ad in *The New York Times* book section . . . and within a year, he had sold over four hundred thousand copies of his book. The book was a tremendous success, and what was once considered an impossible dream, with faith, perseverance, and focused energy, became a highly successful reality!

"Throughout the centuries there have been men who took first steps down new roads armed with nothing but their own vision," wrote Ayn Rand. You have been challenged to resurrect your dreams and, by faith, step out onto a new road that will bring those dreams into reality. And though these steps will not always be easy, in the end, your only regret will be waiting so long to begin.

Seasons of new discovery in life

There are special times over the course of a life when a person discovers, or comprehends for the first time, a profound truth—instances where a person is exposed to, and then begins to grasp, a fundamental reality about life that she never completely understood before. My desire is that this book has done this for you. My hope is you now understand, maybe for the first time, that when you were created, you were given a unique picture of what your life could accomplish and stand for. A dream you now know needs to be fully embraced and pursued.

When you discover a new and profound truth, often it will take a few years to develop the habits, skills, and behaviors needed to fully express this truth in your life. Just because we comprehend a truth does not necessarily mean you will know how to fully incorporate it into your life. Many times fully integrating your new understanding will take years, or maybe even a lifetime to accomplish.

I remember in my own life when I finally understood and embraced, for the first time, the profound proverb: "As a man thinks in his heart, so is he." While I had heard many quotes like this one over the course of my life, it was not until my late thirties that the reality and weight of this statement hit me like a bolt of lightning while sitting on the beach watching the surf. For whatever reason, it was on that day I finally completely comprehended the power of this proverb. (I recall seeing a group of overweight old men walk by me wearing tight Speedo swimsuits. Maybe seeing that group of senior citizens in their tight beachwear shocked my senses so deeply that this reality could finally surface in my mind!)

But even though I now fully embrace the inherent power of my thoughts, it has taken me many *more* years to develop the habits to consistently align my thinking to this fundamental truth. For the art of controlling my thoughts is, even to this day, not easy for me to carry out. Just as it has taken years to develop my gift of writing, so it will take years to develop the skills of thought management in my life.

In a similar fashion, the truths and systems shared in the previous chapters, will take time and discipline to effectively use in your life. This is OK, and to be expected. But now that you understand, maybe for the first time, that your dreams are in your heart for a reason, my challenge is that you now enter into the courageous life, and then forever remain on this quest. Never to falter or retreat.

Your dreams will rise or fall on your belief

As this book draws to a close, I want to return one last time to a fundamental truth emphasized throughout this book because it will forever form the cornerstone of the courageous life. And though this may be one of those truths you are only now discovering and understanding for the first time, it will be one you must continually remind yourself of, and re-embrace in your heart, as you strive to reach new levels of success in any area of your life, including the pursuit of your dreams. And this fundamental truth is this: Everything is possible if you believe.

As mentioned earlier, I believe a fundamental law that governs life is the law of belief. This law states that whatever you believe regarding a specific issue will directly dictate what you experience regarding that issue. It is this same law that drives the phenomenon of self-fulfilling prophecies experienced by many people.

Claude Bristol writes, "Gradually I discovered that there is a golden thread that runs through all the teachings and makes them work for those who sincerely accept and apply them, and that thread can be named in a single word—belief. It is this same element, belief, which causes people to be healed, enables others to climb high the ladder of success, and gets phenomenal results for all who accept it . . . have no doubt about it, there is something magical in believing."

As I sat on that beach a few years ago observing that odd group of men walking by me wearing tightly crafted swimsuits, I finally understood that we make, or unmake, ourselves by the thoughts we cherish. It is in the furnace of your mind that you forge the weapons by which you destroy yourself or fashion the tools to build your success. It is the careful formation of right thoughts that enables you to reach your potential and complete acts of goodness, and it is the abuse of your thoughts that can lead us down to the lowest levels of decadence and evil. A particular and persistent flow of thoughts through your mind —be they good or bad—will never fail to reproduce their fruit on your character and circumstances. And though you may not always *choose* the circumstances you are in, you do have the freedom to choose your thoughts, which in turn have the power to *shape* your circumstances.

A related law that governs humanity and its interactions is: "We reap what we sow." British philosophical thinker and poet James Allen writes, "Good thoughts and actions can never produce bad results; bad thoughts and actions can never produce good results. This is but saying that nothing can come from corn but corn. Men understand this law in the natural world, and work with it; but few understand it in the mental and moral world, though its operation there is just as simple and undeviating."

The concept of cause and effect is found in both Hinduism and Buddhism, where there is a sort of forensic continuity, and that ultimately people do get what they deserve.

While some people do not understand how this law of "cause and effect" impacts their daily lives, there are individuals who proactively strive to incorporate it into their everyday lives. Zig Ziglar writes, "If you don't like who you are and where you are, don't sweat it. You're not stuck there. You can grow. You can change. Just remember that you are what you are and where you are because of what's gone into your mind. You can change what you are and where you are by changing what goes into your mind."

What do you believe? What do you believe about your potential, the potential of your family, and your ability to see this potential realized? Do you believe you can, or can't? Do you believe you will, or you won't? Whatever you believe about a specific matter will eventually attract that reality in your life. This is a profound truth that will impact every area of your life, whether physical, spiritual, emotional, or relational. Your thoughts will powerfully attract into your life whatever beliefs and pictures they focus on . . . for good or for bad.

An example of this law of belief is found in Scripture, in the story of Jonah, a prophet sent by God to inform the great city of Nineveh that it would be destroyed if the people did not repent of their wickedness and sin. Jonah refuses to give Nineveh the message because, deep down, he would love to see the city destroyed, for he personally despises the Ninevites. But after a unique experience with a fish changes Jonah's mind, he reluctantly goes to Nineveh and preaches the apocalyptic warning. Surprisingly, the city repents and God shows mercy on the people and graciously spares the city, but when this happens, Jonah becomes extremely angry and cries out, "O Lord, is this not what I said when I was still at home?" Jonah's fear had become his reality. His archenemy, the Ninevites, had been spared by God. And though there are other factors at play in this story, the fact remains—what Jonah feared would happen . . . happened.

Both thoughts of fear and belief will work to create their reality in your lives. No matter what the thought, the seeds planted from your mental pictures will eventually produce fruit. So, what kind of seeds are you planting in your mind? Are they seeds of fear and doubt, or faith and belief? "If you realized how powerful your thoughts are, you would never think a negative thought," writes Mildred Norman, peace activist.

Forging tools of belief

Now that you understand the importance and power of this law of belief, the following tools will help forge habits that will effectively support such a mindset of belief in your everyday life.

The first and most important tool is to completely embrace the magic and power that belief can have in your life and over your dreams—where you fully embrace the fact that believing in yourself is more important than your knowledge, social status, current skills, or your level of schooling. Did you know that twenty percent of America's millionaires never went to college, 21 of the 222 listed billionaires in America in 2003 never received their college diplomas; and two of those never even finished high school?

So although a commitment to lifelong learning is essential to success, a formal degree is not. Jack Canfield writes, "Even Vice President Dick Cheney dropped out of college. When you realize that the vice president, the richest man in America, and many twenty-million-dollars-a-movie actors, as well as many of your greatest musicians and athletes, are all college dropouts, you see that you can start from anywhere and create a successful life for yourself." In the end, those who reach their dreams are those individuals who firmly believed they could. That is the magic of believing!

The second tool needed to cement the power of belief in your heart and mind is to accept full responsibility for choosing your thoughts and attitude. The only person who can choose your attitude, and whether you believe in yourself and your potential, is you. Viktor Frankl wrote, "Between stimulus and response, there is a space. In that space lies your freedom and your power to choose your response. In your response lies your growth and your happiness."

There is always a space between what happens to us in life, and how we choose to respond to that event. No matter what the circumstance, there is always this space of time where we have the freedom to choose our attitude, behaviors, and whether we will allow a difficult event to beat us, or propel us forward.

When Viktor Frankl spent those years in a concentration camp, it was there he came to his life-changing conclusion that "everything can be taken from a man but . . . the last of the human freedoms—to choose one's attitude—and in any given set of circumstances, to choose one's way." The responsibility to choose to "believe" lies solely and soundly within each of us. It cannot be given to us by another, or transferred by us to someone else.

I know firsthand that there are few things worse than the feeling of malaise that can overcome someone when his self-esteem and confidence is low. But it is during these times that I am faced with a choice—a choice to continue wallowing in my fears and low esteem, or to turn my thoughts toward a renewed belief in myself and in the dreams in my heart. And though this choice is rarely easy, it never fails to lead me out of the valley and back onto the mountaintop where I again can see the many beauties of this world and the many blessings in my life. A quote I keep at the forefront of my mind during these difficult times is "Don't believe everything you hear—even in your own mind." (Daniel G. Amen, psychiatrist and neuroscientist)

This power we have to choose our attitude and belief is reflected in a short poem written on the wall of a concentration camp during World War II. It read:

> I believe in the sun
> even when it is not shining.
> I believe in love
> even when I feel it not.
> I believe in God
> even when He is silent.

Do you *believe* in your potential? Do you *believe* in the dream God has placed in your heart? How you respond to these questions is your choice.

The third tool that is effective in cementing a perspective of belief into your spirit is to develop a few habits and rituals that keep your faith strong. Psychologist Martin Seligman found that a person can consciously change their attitude from doubt to positive belief by learning how to coach her inner dialogue. He notes that "becoming an optimist consists of learning a set of skills about how to talk to yourself when you suffer a personal defeat." If a person is willing, she can develop the tools and habits to change her inner dialogue from words of doubt, to words of encouragement, self-motivation, and faith.

One habit I have found useful is to say to myself each morning, right after I get out of bed: "This is the day that the Lord has made, I will rejoice and be glad in it!" You can use any positive phrase that would motivate you. Saying a phrase such as this one three or four times each morning helps my mind get off to a positive and optimistic start. Even if it's rainy, windy, and cold outside, this statement is a reminder of how each day is a special gift and that I have the freedom to choose whether I will allow the rain, wind, and cold to dampen my spirits, or invigorate my whole body as I step out toward the day.

Another phrase I sometimes repeat is, "I believe something great and good is going to happen to me today!" And later, when I reflect back on my day, I always find this has been true—that many good things indeed happened to me during the day. Another habit is to simply repeat the phrase, "I believe" over and over throughout the day. You will be surprised how repeating these two words can help reenergize and refocus your thoughts toward images of positive faith and belief. It never fails.

Using an expression such as this one is intrinsic to many religious and spiritual traditions and helps to focus the mind, heart, and body when repeated with focus and attention. Simple phrases (or mantras) like this can quiet your soul, even at odd moments of the day, and help refocus you on your dreams. The term "mantra" is derived from two roots: "man," to think; and the action-oriented suffix "tra." Thus a mantra can help focus one's thoughts, and aid in aligning your *self* with your *purpose.*

I also place icons in various places that are specifically intended to remind me of the dreams God has placed in my heart. A few years ago, while staying at the condo of a good friend, I was sitting on the beach when the idea to write this book first drifted into my mind. But since that day, there have been times when I have doubted the legitimacy of this dream and have had misgivings regarding my ability to accomplish the dream. So one thing I have done is to place a seashell from that beach on the dash of my Jeep. Now, whenever I drive, I am reminded of that clear summer day when I was first inspired to write this book. From time to time, just looking at that white seashell reminds me to believe—and to have faith in the dream that (as of this writing) is still yet to be completed.

In addition to these icons, the habit of reviewing my goals every day, along with the steps I need to take toward my dream, helps to refocus my thoughts and attitude. Reviewing my action plan helps take my eyes off my current situation and refocus them on the horizon that is being illuminated by the first lights of my dream and goals being accomplished. They are a constant reminder that I do not have to give in to my present circumstances, but have the freedom to choose where my life is headed.

Another idea: spend time with people who are optimistic about life and who believe in their own dreams. If you are struggling with feelings of doubt, spend fifteen dollars on your dream by taking a person out for lunch, someone you know is optimistic and filled with faith. Just hanging out with them for an hour or so will go a long way to reignite the fire and passion in your life. Successful people maintain a positive perspective in life, no matter what is going on around them, and their ability to stay focused on the future, instead of past failures, will help you do the same.

Finally, spend the last few minutes before you fall asleep recalling the ways you were personally blessed during the day, making note of everything you are thankful for. Also, take a minute to form a positive mental picture of the dream you are currently pursuing.

A friend uses the following acronym as a guide to review his day. After he has put his kids to bed for the night, he takes out his journal and writes down along one side of a page the letters *B, A, G, E, L,* and *S* (spelling the word "bagels"). Alongside each letter he writes in his journal a one-sentence response to the question each letter represents. The acronym is as follows:

B (Behavior)—What is my goal for tomorrow?

A (Attitude)—How do you feel about yourself? (Write in the present tense)

G (Major Goals)—What are the major goals I am presently focused on?

E (Key Experiences)—What was the key experience of the day?

L (Lesson Learned)—What was the lesson learned during the day?

S (Success)—What was the success of the day?

Taking ten minutes to complete such a list each night will help refocus your mind on how you are growing and where your life is positively headed.

In 1977, in Tallahassee, Florida, Laura Shultz, who was sixty-three years old, picked up the back end of a car to lift it off her grandson's arm. Before that time, she had never lifted anything heavier than a fifty-pound bag of pet food. Dr. Charles Garfield, author of *Peak Performance* and *Peak Performers,* went to interview Laura after this event, and when he got to her home, she kept resisting any attempts to talk about what she called "the event." She kept asking Dr. Garfield to eat some breakfast and call her "Granny" instead—which he did.

When he finally got her to talk about "the event," she said she did not like to think about it because it challenged her beliefs about what she could and could not do, and about what was really possible. She said, "If I was able to do this when I didn't think I could, what does that say about the rest of my life? Have I wasted it?"

Dr. Garfield convinced her that her life was not yet over and that she could still do whatever she wanted to do. He then asked her about her dream. She mentioned she loved rocks and had always wanted to study geology, but her parents did not have enough money to send both her and her brother to college, so her brother was the only one who got to go. So at sixty-three, with a little encouragement and coaching from Dr. Garfield, she decided to go back to school to study geology. She eventually received her degree and went on to teach at a local community college.

Though believing in yourself is a choice and an attitude that will need to be developed over time, always remember it is *your* responsibility to take charge of your thoughts and attitude. Don't expect someone to do it for you, or for your thoughts to mysteriously change on their own. Create your future by choosing to believe in yourself and your dreams.

The tools of effective barrier breaking

The first portion of this chapter discussed the critical importance of maintaining a mindset of belief as you move away from your comfort zone and step toward your courageous dreams. We will conclude this chapter by discussing a few thoughts on how to effectively overcome the barriers that will surely cross your path as you make your journey.

No matter how skilled you are, as you reach toward a new dream, you will inevitably experience frustration and setbacks along the way which, if not handled carefully, can cause you to give up on your dream and retreat to living a mediocre life.

Johnny Unitas was one of the greatest quarterbacks to ever play in the National Football League (NFL); he was also inducted into the NFL Hall of Fame. But the path leading to his dream of playing in the NFL was riddled with obstacles and detours. His father died at a young age, and his mother was left to care for her children by working numerous jobs—doing everything from cleaning offices to delivering coal. Johnny, though small, dreamed of playing football after high school, but no university would offer him a scholarship, so he went off to play for a small college instead. After completing college, his dream turned to playing in the NFL. He tried out for his home team, the Pittsburgh Steelers, but was cut from the roster of players in very short order. He then went out and found a construction job building skyscrapers in downtown Pittsburgh, all the while holding on to his dream of someday playing professional football. He did not view himself as a victim of his circumstances, but as someone who would succeed despite his size, or any other barrier.

After reviewing his options, Johnny decided he was willing to start anywhere. So he found a small league that paid him six dollars a game, which allowed him to improve his football skills while staying in touch with various NFL teams, in a hope that one day he would be noticed. After seven months of honing his skills, he received an invitation to try out for the Baltimore Colts . . . and the rest is history. Johnny Unitas went on to become one of the greatest quarterbacks to ever play in the National Football League.

Jack Canfield writes that "persistence is probably the single most common quality of high achievers. They simply refuse to give up." No matter what obstacles we may face along the way, we must never give up on our dreams. Consider this:

✳ Admiral Robert Peary attempted to reach the North Pole seven times before he finally reached the Pole on his eighth try.

✳ In its first twenty-eight attempts to send a rocket into space, NASA failed twenty times.

✳ On board a ship from England, Gail Borden saw children die as a result of drinking contaminated milk. This experience impacted his life in such a way that he dedicated his life to finding a way for people to drink milk safely. After many failed attempts he saw how the Shakers in New York condensed maple sugar in a vacuum-sealed pan, so he tried a similar method for storing milk. His success led to the safety of milk in a non-refrigerated world, and launched the modern dairy industry. On his tombstone are the following words of perseverance, "I tried and failed. I tried again and succeeded."

Overcoming the barriers you will face when pursuing a dream will not be easy. But again, there are tools you can forge that can help you effectively overcome whatever obstacles you do happen to face along the way.

One tool you need to forge is to fully *expect* and *accept* that difficult times and obstacles will cross your path at various points in the courageous life. You need to accept that this is a common experience with which everyone who has ever pursued a dream has dealt.

When you first formulate a dream, and then create a plan to help get you there, many times you will experience such a high level of confidence and excitement that you believe nothing can stop you from accomplishing the dream. But as time goes by, and as reality starts to smack you square in the face, you may become bewildered and frustrated as raindrops of doubt start to sprinkle on your dream. If you are not careful, this sprinkle of doubt can eventually grow into a raging storm that can completely snuff out the embers of what was once a burning passion in your heart.

While in high school, I went out to Colorado with my brother and some friends over Spring Break. I had never snow skied before, but thought that since I could water-ski it would be relatively easy to learn. I had visions of grandeur of skiing down the white-powdered mountainside, impressing the numerous girls I would inevitably pass on my way down to the ski lodge.

Well, my first day on the slopes was a complete fiasco. I could not go more than a few feet without falling down, losing my skies, and getting icy snow down my backside. And I was absolutely impressing no girls in the process. To be quite honest, I was very close to giving up and taking off my gear when my older brother said, "Come with me and I will help you learn how to ski, real fast." My brother had been skiing for a few years, and so I followed him to one of the chairlifts leading up into the misty clouds covering the mountaintop that day. After a fifteen-minute ride straight up, I got off the chairlift and immediately fell down, causing the lift to come to a stop while I picked up my gear.

My brother then proceeded to take me to a black-diamond slope and said, "Here you go. This will help you learn how to ski, real fast." So I took him at his word, and started down the slope as he left me by myself. For the next three hours I worked my way down the mountain, slowly learning along the way. While struggling down the ski run, I received help from skiers who yelled suggestions as they passed me by, or rode on the ski lift that was just over my head. I distinctly remember one person saying to a friend as they rode the ski lift, "Man, that guy is going to kill himself."

Well, I did manage to get down the slope that day, while also learning a few basics on how to ski with ever increasing control and speed. And though I never picked up a girl the entire time I was in Colorado, I was glad that I pushed through my frustrations, fears, and lack of ability and taught myself how to ski. The last four days on the slopes provided memories I have never forgotten, and by the end of the third day I was even keeping up with my brother!

As with any new endeavor, when pursuing a dream, we will experience times of frustration along the way. At these times the journey will be difficult, but if we are ready and fully expect these difficulties to occur, we will be in a better posture to learn whatever lessons are needed to enable us to continue moving toward our dream.

Another tool for effective barrier breaking is to specifically and accurately clarify the nature of the difficulty you face. Pin it down. Make sure you are dealing with a real obstacle and not something you have imagined in your mind. When Martha and I bought our first home, I personally did not think we were financially ready to take on the commitment of a mortgage and additional upkeep for a home. My income working in a not-for-profit ministry was not large, and I did not believe we could make it work. But at my wife's encouragement and prodding, I agreed to investigate various options and opportunities for first-time home buyers, and the more information and facts we uncovered, the more we realized that purchasing a home was doable. My preconceived belief about our inability to wisely purchase a home was a "feeling" not based on fact. I had created a barrier to our dream out of what I *felt* was true, not out of what *was* the truth.

Even when an obstacle is real, if you take the time to accurately define what the obstacle is (and is not), then you will have the clarity to make much wiser decisions regarding how to best overcome that barrier. When I decided to start my own consulting business, one of the most significant barriers to overcome was how to create new streams of income that would adequately support the needs of my family and new business.

So to help accurately define this barrier, the first thing I did was to study my budget and clearly identify what my income need would be. After the amount was determined, my "barrier" was rightly defined. And as I finished the process of clearly defining this barrier, an exciting thing happened . . . my dream began to appear more and more doable, for the financial barrier ended up being smaller than I originally "felt" it would be. In addition, once this figure was defined, it enabled me to wisely plan how to secure those new sources of income. Then slowly, as new consulting clients were found, this barrier faded into the foggy mist.

Leadership expert Max Depree writes that "the first responsibility of a leader is to define reality," and it will only be after we have taken time to accurately define what a barrier is (and is not), that we will be able to effectively attack that barrier.

Another tool enabling you to traverse difficult times is to stay focused on moving forward one step at a time. Whenever you face a clearly defined barrier, take one step into that barrier and see what happens. Usually you will find that as you take a few steps into a barrier or fear, it will slowly start to dissipate.

For example, when my wife and I began to take steps toward the purchase of a new home by researching various options, the obstacles started to become smaller and smaller until they became completely manageable. The same was true when I started my own consulting business. Once my income needs were defined, I proceeded to take steps to find clients who could provide that revenue. And as potential organizations were contacted who could benefit from my services, I eventually reached a point where the finances were no longer an obstacle at all. And so it will be true for your dreams if you will just start, and then continue, to take specific steps of faith into whatever barrier is in your path.

Martin Luther King Jr. said, "Take the first step in faith. You don't have to see the whole staircase. Just take the first step." The practice of taking a step into a barrier, fear, or obstacle enables you to start dealing with that issue—for until you take that first step, you will find yourself feeling more and more de-energized as you just stare at the obstacle. Nobel laureate Rabindranath Tagore noted, "You can't cross a sea by merely staring into the water." Be willing to enter the unknown waters, choose to set sail and trust that your next port will appear on the horizon. It will.

Another option is to seek wise counsel regarding how to most effectively approach a difficult issue. The book of Proverbs teaches that "Plans fail for lack of counsel, but with many advisers they succeed," and "For lack of guidance a nation falls, but many advisors make victory sure."

Remember, there is nothing new under the sun. There will never be anything you face in life that others have not already dealt with in some form or setting. And if you actively seek them out, these people can provide invaluable guidance and counsel as you attempt to traverse the same issue in your own life. Therefore, whenever you find yourself facing a seemingly insurmountable wall, seek out the expert advice of someone who can help you look at the situation from a new perspective and provide insights on how to best overcome that barrier.

As mentioned earlier, some of the most valuable wisdom, help, and advice a person will ever get need only cost the price of a meal, if they will just invite a wise sage out to lunch for some good food and advice.

As a young child, whenever I would struggle to remove the lid from the candy jar sitting on our kitchen counter, my parents would always help out by advising me to "try turning the lid the other way" and you know what, this always worked. Being much older and wiser, and having taken off many more lids than I had, the advice of my parents always allowed me to stop straining and easily uncover the riches of candy contained in that glass container. And so will the advice of others help to free you from whatever barriers you face as you pursue a dream.

Just this past week, I managed to break off a lug nut while changing the front tire on my car. Besides being surprised by my brute strength (or embarrassed that I still do not know which way to turn something to loosen it), I tried to figure out how to fix it. I spent an hour looking on the Internet for instructions on how to replace a lug nut, and when I found nothing on the Web, I hit the wheel a few times with a hammer, and when that didn't work, decided to just sell the car. But I then remembered a mechanic who could help me with this problem, and sure enough he fixed the lug nut with ease, and in very little time.

Whenever you face a significant struggle, get help. Don't sell the car, or give up on your dream. Remember that there is nothing new under the sun, and then find someone who has experience and knowledge to help you overcome the specific issue you happen to face. Buy them a Coke, and humbly seek their guidance and help.

A FINAL THOUGHT

The courageous life is one filled with tensions and paradoxes. While the courageous life is invigorating and exciting, it is also a formidable challenge. And though pursuing your dreams will be a lonely experience at times, your dreams will never be achieved without the help of others. And though this pursuit will eventually lead toward your potential, it will always require that you first leave your comfort zone . . . and never go back. The journey will challenge the limits of your faith, but will never exceed your capacity to believe. And though it may hurt at times, it will never leave you with regrets. It is a life that entices the masses, yet only a few will choose to follow its call. The courageous life gives life. The ordinary life is a slow death, or at best, a life filled with lukewarm hopes and distant desires.

All through this book the challenge has been to turn off the main thoroughfare and walk down the narrower path leading in a new direction. To turn onto a pathway that too many people choose to pass on by. It is a path that may lead into the wilderness, but it is also the path that will allow you to reach the summit of your dreams.

My challenge to you is to not only choose the right path, but to wisely use the tools which will help you effectively travel that path. For both the right path *and* the right tools will be needed to successfully complete this journey. Just as digging with the right tools in the wrong location will never produce the gold a person is looking for—digging in the *right* place with the *right* tools will never fail to produce a bountiful reward! The tools detailed in this chapter, and book, are the right tools—and the right place to use these tools is at the precise location of your courageous dream.

The following chapter will discuss one final critical question . . . *What next?* When you finally reach your dream, where do you go after that? Is your courageous journey over?

CHAPTER 9

Dream Until Your Dreams Come True

Fewer than 10 percent of all books are read past the first two chapters. So if you are reading these words, and have made it this far in this book, congratulations! You have remained committed to the entire process of educating yourself on the numerous aspects of the courageous life. You have courageously stepped out to clarify your dream and have created a personalized action plan to help you move toward that dream. By doing all this, you have chosen to join the elite few who have turned off the main thoroughfare of life to journey on a path leading through the wilderness and up to the mountaintop of their dream.

Believe me, when you finally reach the summit, there will be nowhere else you would rather be standing. Everyone who has reached the Mount Everest of their dream will attest to this fact, for there are few experiences better than the feeling of elation which will rush through your body when you finally stand at the summit of your dream!

This final chapter will offer a few concluding remarks regarding what you will experience as you continue on this courageous quest. Namely, what can you expect in the future? Will you be successful? Will you ever finish your courageous journey? And when you successfully attain your dream, then what? Where do you go from there?

Entering my final semester of undergraduate work at the University of Illinois, I discovered there were two "free" hours of credit that could be used to take any class I wanted. Since I had been hammering away for four long years in various engineering courses, I decided to use these two free hours of credit to take a totally different type of class—a class on weightlifting. I have always valued physical fitness in my life, and believed this class would help beef up my lean and lanky body. I had just seen an Arnold Schwarzenegger movie and had a mental picture of totally transforming my body into a muscle-making, girl-attracting machine!

So during that last semester of college, I went twice each week to my weightlifting class envisioning the physical transformation that awaited me in that musty old weight room. Throughout the semester, I faithfully attended each class, drank protein shakes, and counted my reps carefully. And now, some twenty-five years later, though I never attained the body of Arnold Schwarzenegger or Hulk Hogan, the habit that started back in the spring of 1984 has remained. Since then I have continued to exercise on a regular basis. In fact, there have only been a few weeks over the years where I have not pushed around a barbell of some kind. So in the end, my dream back in 1984 to create a body like the Hulk (minus the green skin) led to a lifestyle of physical fitness which has provided significant benefits for my health ever since.

Please understand that the courageous life does not *only* lead a person to the destination of their dreams; more importantly, it shifts a person's whole perspective on how they should live their life. Similar to how my goal in college to attain a body like Arnold Schwarzenegger eventually changed my mindset to live an entire *life* of physical fitness, my hope is that in the end, pursuing a courageous dream will forever change your perspective on how you live your *entire* life.

When a person commits to the courageous life, he is embracing a new mindset where he begins to look at their future through the lens of faith, belief, and reaching ever-new levels of potential. When you started reading this book, you were simply challenged to uncover, and embrace, your heartfelt dreams. But as you have moved through this process, the challenge grew to not only embrace your dreams, but to embrace a mindset where you will *forever* strive to pursue loftier dreams and reach newer heights.

Now that you have accepted that challenge, I want to say a few closing words about the general topic of success, followed by a three-fold challenge:

THE FIVE THEMES OF SUCCESS

People who reach high levels of success have a compelling determination and ability to excel in five interconnected areas of their life:

1. They each have **extreme clarity** regarding their life purpose, dreams, and goals. These people have clearly defined who they are, and what they want to achieve.

2. They have a **firm belief** in both who they are and in the dreams (and goals) they are moving toward. They have chosen to believe in what they do not yet see.

3. Successful people are always **taking action**. They determine what specific steps need to be taken to reach their dream—and then set out to take those steps . . . often into the unknown. Their fear of not realizing their dream is *greater* than the perceived cost of not reaching that dream.

4. Throughout their personal journey toward success **they respect the greatest law** that governs life, the law of love. While these people may be successful, they also take the initiative to express love to others along the way. They actively love God, themselves, and others in their life.

5. Finally, though not perfect, highly successful people work hard to **protect their integrity** and maintain their **character** in their life and business.

The contents of this book have already dealt with the first three themes of success in detail, but before finishing this book, I want to briefly discuss the final two ingredients:

THE GREATEST LAW

While working in youth ministry, I would often tell teenagers that if they wanted to obey the entire Bible, then all they needed to do is obey two simple (though not easy) commands. The first command is to "Love God with all your heart, soul, mind and strength" and the second is to "Love your neighbor as yourself." Other religions follow the same precepts, for example in Confucianism, the edict is "Do not do to others what you do not want them to do to you," and in Hinduism, it is written "One should not behave toward others in a way which is disagreeable to oneself."

People I have known who were facing their imminent death have expressed at least some regret around two themes. The first is for not having taken more steps of faith to pursue their dreams and potential. The second theme is for not having taken more time to actively love their spouse, children, parents, friends, their God, and others during their short life.

Rick Warren, author of *The Purpose-Driven Life,* writes that there are five fundamental truths about living a successful and significant life. Rick writes that if we fail to actively love others: nothing we say will matter; nothing we know will ultimately matter; nothing we believe will ultimately matter; nothing we give will matter; and nothing we accomplish in life will ultimately matter. For without love, your words are just noise, your knowledge is flawed, your beliefs are superficial, your gifts are selfishly motivated, and your accomplishments are (at best) only of temporary value.

Don't fool yourself—the only way you can live a life of lasting significance and meaning is when your work, relationships, and even your dreams are all founded on a sincere love for yourself and for those around you. Mother Teresa once said, "The greatest science in the world; in heaven and on earth; is love." And through her many years of serving the poor and needy, she noted, "There is more hunger for love and appreciation in this world than for bread."

Brian Tracy writes, "Always, love is the answer. The only thing that you can never have enough of is love. You can never have too much love for yourself, and you can never give too much love to others. Lack of love, or love withheld, lies at the root of most personal and behavioral problems. Love is not only the answer, but it is the cure for most of life's problems."

The supreme law that governs everything else is the law of love, for life is ultimately about love, and true success is ultimately based on love. Make no mistake about it, you will find that the accomplishment of a dream will leave you deeply unsatisfied if it was not founded upon, and reached in a manner which reflected a sincere love and concern for others along the way. If you truly want to be successful in everything you do, if you want the accomplishment of your dreams to leave a positive and lasting legacy of who you were, then study, practice, and become an expert in the art of loving your Creator, yourself, and those around you.

Though I deeply believe in the power of love, I have found that loving other people does not come naturally, nor will it come naturally for you. This is because we are all inherently programmed to think of ourselves first and to focus on meeting our own needs, many times without regard for how it may affect others.

I mentioned in an earlier chapter that my natural tendency is to hide our yearly allotment of Girl Scout cookies in a place where I can have them to myself. Now, your issue may not be Girl Scout cookies, but each one of us has a natural inclination to focus on our own needs, wants, and desires, even at the expense of those we care about. I am reminded of my inclination to dominate the remote control whenever we are watching a "family" night of television. Over the years, I have learned the art of channel surfing in a way that allows me to shrewdly pass over the home decorating channels to shows I would rather watch . . . like a good old action movie or World War II documentary.

Therefore, since life is ultimately about love, the ultimate work in life is to *learn* how to love others more deeply and consistently. I have found that the best way to grow in my ability to love others is to first realize that love is a choice, not a feeling. Love is something we do, not something we always feel. I have found that my ability to love others will start to grow as I simply start to share it with others. Remember, love is an act of the will, and as you continue to express love to those around you, you will begin to see your capacity to love grow stronger and stronger until it starts to impact larger and larger circles of people around you. It will be then that you will have combined life's ultimate meaning (to love) in a way which also honors your ultimate mission (to pursue your God-given dreams).

THE GREATEST SAFEGUARD IN LIFE!

Though highly successful people have extreme clarity about what they want to achieve, believe in both who they are and in what they want to accomplish, and consistently take action while expressing love to others along the way—highly successful people are also very careful to protect their integrity and maintain their character in both their personal and professional life. Successful people understand that their integrity is a primary protector, and sustainer, of whatever level of success they ultimately achieve. Successful people understand what Heraclites wrote in 500 BC: "A man's character is his fate."

As you step out toward a dream, understand that if you ever plan to experience the intense and untainted joy of reaching the summit of that dream, then you will need to carefully protect your character as you make your journey to the top. Your life will reap the fruit of the conduct and behavior we sow along the way, as reflected in this anonymous poem:

Be careful of your thoughts, for your thoughts become your words;

Be careful of your words, for your words become your deeds;

Be careful of your deeds, for your deeds become your habits;

Be careful of your habits; for your habits become your character;

Be careful of your character; for your character becomes your destiny.

Over the course of time, your choices and behaviors will shape your character, and your character will then determine who you become and the kind of impact your accomplishments will have on those around you. Your character is not something you can fashion overnight; it must be earned and proven over time—built brick by brick, through the weeks, months, and years of life. As historian James A. Froude wrote, "You cannot dream yourself into a character; you must hammer and forge yourself one."

So, how strong is your character? What comments do you think your friends are making about your integrity? Where would family members see cracks in your integrity? What habits and behaviors in your life have you kept hidden through the years, hoping no one will find them out? And the most important question to ask yourself is "Do you really believe maintaining your character and integrity is of primary importance in your life?" If so, why? If not, why not?

If you do not believe protecting your character is of critical importance, then I challenge you to consider people you personally know who consistently compromise their integrity and character. What kind of fruit is their life producing? As I consider these people in my life, I do not know of one person who has lived a life of compromise; who has also maintained a long-term, happy, and growing marriage with their partner; who currently has the deep respect of their adult children; or who is truly admired as a role model of success by their peers.

While no person is perfect, we can divide humanity into two major groups. One group realizes their frailty, are aware of their personal vices, and are on a lifelong journey to manage and correct those breaches of integrity in their living. The second group is also on a lifelong journey. But their goal is to forever hide and cover up these breaches as they continue to indulge in their vices and addictive behaviors—hoping never to be found out.

I have spent time in both of these groups, and know from personal experience that when we choose to hide and indulge our vices, we are forced to spend so much energy protecting ourselves from being found out that inadequate energy and creative power is left to pursue the courageous life. So we are forced to choose. Chase your vices, or chase your dreams.

If you are living a lie and condoning an ethical breech in your character, you will not have the ability to sustain the high levels of energy and focus needed to reach the summit of your dream. And make no doubt about it; you will not be the exception to this rule. We are all forced to choose. We are all forced to choose between pursuing the courageous life and living a risky lie.

So as you pursue your dreams, and other visions of success for your life, make certain that you carefully watch over and protect your inner soul and integrity. Fully embrace the fact that you first need to *be* the right kind of person, and *do* the right kinds of things, before you will excel in reaching your potential.

Zig Ziglar tells of a salesperson whose life reflects this fundamental truth. "Cadillac Jack's" advertisement to potential customers starts with the question:

Do you know a car salesman who will:

✻ Take you to the airport and have your car serviced while you are away?

✻ Have your car picked up at your home or business for service?

✻ Have a loaner car supplied to you when your car is in for warranty work?

✻ Provide you with a mobile phone number or beeper when your car is in for service?

✻ Have your car towed whenever with you get stuck or have an accident?

Bring keys to you if you get locked out or lose your keys?

 Bring you up to five gallons of fuel if you run out?

 Jump-start your battery for any reason?

 Come out and change your tire if it goes flat?

 Help you plan a trip and reimburse you for expenses for hotels, meals, and rental cars if your trip is interrupted for warranty failure and your car has to be put in the shop for repair?

 Have your car washed when it is in for service?

 Have your car tags renewed?

Cadillac Jack closes his questionnaire by saying, "As your personal transportation specialist, you will be able to call me by cell phone or at my home any time. I will personally see that you get these services . . ." and his reputation for following through has been firmly established. Make no mistake about it; Jack's good heart and integrity have propelled him to the highest levels of success. He clearly demonstrates that you have to be the right kind of person, and do the right things, before you will reap the benefits of a highly successful life.

No matter where life takes you, no matter what you see others doing around you . . . guard your character. Be a person others can trust. Plant seeds of integrity wherever you go and you will eventually reap a bountiful crop of personal respect, success, and satisfaction. Let your integrity not only lead you, but also protect you on your journey to the top.

Here are three final challenges regarding your courageous journey: 1) to continually dream new dreams, 2) to be a champion of the courageous life to those around you, and 3) from here on out never retreat back into living just a common and mediocre existence.

1 Continually dream new dreams

The courageous life is a journey and not a destination. There will always be new dreams to pursue and new heights of potential to be realized. As I find myself close to completing my dream of writing this book, my thoughts have started to turn to the question: "What next?"

In the athletic world, there is a phenomena known as "post-Olympic syndrome." Athletic research has found that many Olympic athletes experience a significant period of depression after competing in the Olympic Games. After the Games are over, these athletes go through a period of malaise where they do not want to train, find it hard to focus, and struggle to know what to do next. Having just completed years of intense training to attain a specific goal, they find it difficult to answer the question: "*What next?*"

In similar fashion, an individual can experience "post-dream syndrome." These individuals have spent months, maybe years, expending significant amounts of time and energy to pursue a courageous vision, and after they have attained the summit of their dream, are unprepared for life afterwards.

But the solution to "post-dream syndrome" is simple. All a person needs to do is to keep their list of Potential Future Dreams constantly updated in their journal. And then, when they find themselves nearing the accomplishment of a current dream, to take time away to pray and ponder which dream they will chase next. Which compelling dream will they embrace, pursue, and use to lead them into the future—allowing them to reach ever-new levels of satisfaction and personal accomplishment.

No matter what stage of life you are in, to live without a compelling dream is to slowly wither and die. This may sound overstated, but it is the truth. Living without a dream, without something that engulfs your focus, time, passion, and energy, will cause your life to slowly shrivel up from the inside out.

There are many reasons why people die before the proper time . . .

a poor diet, not being physical fit, and addictive habits are just a few reasons why an individual might die young. But research has shown that the surest way to meet a premature death is to retire from your job with no clear or meaningful purpose for your life. Research has found that the average life span of a person who retires at age sixty-five is eighteen months! So throughout life, no matter what your age, never cease to dream. Never quit pursuing the courageous life. And when a dream is achieved, recommit yourself to that next adventure contained somewhere in your journal, under your list of potential dreams.

Viktor Frankl wrote: "We must never be content with what has already been achieved. Life never ceases to put new questions to us, never permits us to come to rest. . . . The man who stands still is passed by; the man who is smugly contented loses himself. Neither in creating or experiencing may we rest content with achievement; every day, every hour makes new deeds necessary and new experiences possible."

Remember, it is not that you *have to* pursue your dreams. It is you *get to* pursue your dreams. Each of you has an assortment of dreams in your heart, and in addition to these dreams, the ability to achieve them if you are willing to combine your skills with sincere faith and belief.

So when you finally reach a dream . . . dream again. Continue to live a life where you are forever reaching toward the summit of your next Mount Everest. Never stop and forever stay young. Forever stay truly alive!

2 Be a champion of the courageous life to others

The second thought I want to leave with you is, to be a champion of the courageous life to those around you. Continually look for people who you can encourage and help as they step away from their comfort zone to pursue their own dreams and passions. Help others to turn off the crowded thoroughfare leading to mediocrity and discover the path leading to their own Mount Everest.

And just as you needed the support of others when you got started on your courageous journey, look for ways you can help others get started too—and then continue to cheer them on. Look for ways to give encouragement, counsel, feedback, and embolden their faith. And though there will always be individuals who will ignore your plea, choose to be a champion for those who *are* willing to heed the call of the courageous life. Be a champion for the next generation of courageous dreamers and pilgrims who have made the bold choice to set out toward the horizon of a dream.

Pastor and writer Max Lucado writes: "All of us need help sometimes. This journey gets steep. So steep that some of us give up. Some stop climbing. Some just sit down. They are still near the trail but aren't on it. They haven't abandoned the trip, but they haven't continued it. . . . They have simply stopped walking. Much time is spent sitting around the fire, talking about how things used to be. Some will sit in the same place for years. They will not change. Prayers will not deepen. Devotion will not increase. Passion will not rise. A few even grow cynical. Woe to the traveler who challenges them to resume the journey. Woe to the prophet who dares them to see the mountain. Woe to the explorer who reminds them of their call . . . pilgrims are not welcome here. And so the pilgrim moves on while the settler settles. Settles for sameness. Settles for safety. Settles for snowdrifts. I hope you don't do that. But if you do, I hope you don't scorn the pilgrim who calls you back to the journey."

I dare you to be one of those explorers, one of those pilgrims who confidently challenge the "settlers" living around you to get up and set out on their own courageous journey. Be a champion who emboldens others to not settle for sameness or safety, but to instead keep moving up the mountain toward the summit of a dream. Help others believe; to embrace faith. Help them to step through their fears and whatever barrier is in their way.

As you challenge the settlers around you, make sure that you never sugarcoat the work and sacrifice it will take to live the courageous life. Resist the temptation to make the courageous journey something it is not. The pursuit of your dreams will not be easy, nor will it be easy for those who follow us. But always remember, in some ironic way, it is the challenge that makes the journey so special and invigorating. It is in the conquering of the giants we face along the way that make this life so fulfilling and rich.

Antarctic explorer Ernest Shackleton, who was putting together a team of explorers to make the first-ever attempt to cross the South Pole on foot, posted this advertisement in 1913: "Men wanted for hazardous journey. Small wages. Bitter cold. Long months of complete darkness. Constant danger. Safe return doubtful. Honor and recognition in case of success." For the twenty-six open slots on his team, Ernest Shackleton had over five thousand applicants!

Now, as in 1913, people are looking for a meaningful and momentous challenge. People are hungry for a chance to live life to the fullest and to experience what only a few individuals will ever get to see and feel. In the pages of this book, you have been given a clear challenge. And in doing so, I have been honest with you regarding both the benefits and costs of the courageous life. And thought the benefits totally outweigh any cost, the journey toward your dream will not be easy. But whatever challenge is faced, it will pale in comparison to the bounty you will receive when the adventure is completed.

So as you move forward in the pursuit of your own dreams, be a champion for those who want to follow you in this quest. Wave and beckon others to join you all along the way. Invite these new pilgrims to attend your "courageous society" group (chapter seven). Embolden them to take their first steps in a new direction.

3 Never retreat, never quit

Finally, I want leave you with the challenge never to retreat. General George Patton, one of the most successful battlefield generals in U.S. history, once proclaimed: "Do ever in all things your damnedest, and never, oh never, retreat." The general also quipped, "I never retreat. I just start fighting in a different direction."

As you pursue your dream, be willing to sacrifice and go after your dream with the same determination of a boxer, who goes into a ring knowing the other guy will try to knock him out. Just like that champion boxer, never retreat back into the ropes; always continue to fight for your dream; never give up.

Dreamers believe in their dreams and develop the tenacity to never quit and never give up. One example of this type of determination is President Abraham Lincoln. Despite business failures, great personal loss, rejection, political defeat, severe financial difficulties, and tremendous emotional and family struggles, Abraham Lincoln ascended to the highest position of government when elected into the office of president of the United States in 1860. From a log cabin to the White House, from poverty to the presidency, Lincoln overcame many obstacles by choosing to believe in himself and resolving that he would never give up. The timeline of Abraham Lincoln's life is one of tenacious determination:

1818   His mother died.

1831   Failed in business.

1832   Defeated as a candidate for state legislature.

1832   Lost his job.

1832   Applied to law school but was denied entrance.

1833   Started a business that went bankrupt. He then spent the next seventeen years paying off the debt.

1835   His fiancée and sweetheart died. (A few years later he proposed to another lady and was turned down.)

1836   Suffered a nervous breakdown.

1838   Sought to become speaker of legislature and was defeated.

1843   Defeated for Congress.

1848   Defeated for Congress.

1849   Attempted to be appointed to the U.S. land office, but was rejected.

1854   Defeated as a candidate for the United States Senate.

1856   Defeated as a candidate for vice president.

1858   Defeated as a candidate for the United States Senate.

1859   His two sons Eddie (age 3) and Willie (age 12) died.

1860   Elected president of the United States.

Another example from history is that of Winston Churchill. As prime minister of the United Kingdom during World War II, each day he would take to the radio airwaves and encourage the Brits to "never, never, never, never give up." He once stated, "This may be your darkest hour, but this may also be your finest hour, because it will show what we really are made of. So never, never, never, give up! Never yield to force. Never yield to the apparently overwhelming might of the enemy."

As a young child, my father took me and my older brother up into the mountains of Colorado for an overnight camping trip. It was an experience I have never forgotten. We climbed up until we found a deserted railroad track carved along the side of a mountain. We then proceeded to walk down the abandoned railway collecting old rail spikes and looking for Indian arrowheads—while also cautiously listening for the rumbling of an oncoming steam locomotive. (The rail tracks had long been abandoned, but my father kept our imaginations peaked with the "possibility" of seeing an old steam train passing by!)

All day we followed those old tracks through numerous turns and abandoned train tunnels, and before dark set up camp inside one of the tunnels, building a fire just outside its opening. We cooked whatever food Mom had prepared for us, ate some candy bars, and told stories around the campfire. All the while, I was keeping my ears perked for the whistle of an old steam train that, if we were not careful, might rush over us as it steamed through the tunnel.

I remember not getting much sleep that night, being continually startled by the noise of a possible train in the distance, or bandits entering the tunnel from the opposite end. But we survived the night and in the morning I felt I had just completed one of the all-time epic adventures of my life. I had braved sleeping in an old train tunnel way up in the mountains with my brother and father, and was also coming home with a bounty of old railroad spikes and an assortment of rocks that at least looked like Indian arrowheads.

While sleeping in the train tunnel that night, there were times when I wanted to pack up and go home to my warm and safe bed. But I chose to remain. Even though I feared getting run over by a train, or robbed by a group of lawless bandits, deep down in my heart I did not want to retreat to safer ground. Deep down I wanted to live the adventure. So I stayed put in the tunnel, and when we walked off that mountain the next morning, I was proud of myself—proud that I had bravely withstood all the night had thrown my way.

So it is in the courageous life. I challenge you to never give up. Never retreat. Don't leave and go home early. Keep pursuing your dream through the dark times, for in the morning you will be proud that you stood strong and bravely endured until the dawn of a new day.

CONGRATULATIONS HEROIC DREAMER AND FRIEND!

Congratulations for completing this detailed study of the courageous life and embracing its challenge to step away from the mediocre life and onto a new path leading to your dreams. This book, and others like it, will serve as a guide to which you can often refer as you make progress in your epic journey.

Remember that you will never be completely alone in this journey, for there will always be a special group of pilgrims around you (including myself) who are also committed to this type of life. I will be sure to encourage you in your quest whenever our paths cross, and please do the same for me whenever we meet along the way.

In addition, remember that God has a special place in his heart for people like us. He holds in high regard those who have chosen to step away from their comfort zone and pursue a life of faith, where they have chosen to believe in who they are and in the dream He has placed in their heart. Watch for God to come along side you with both encouragement and help. Watch, for this will occur.

In my personal journal are various quotes I have read or heard through the years. The first citation, on the very first page of my journal, is a favorite quote:

> "The moment one definitely commits oneself, then Providence moves too. All sorts of things occur to help one that would never otherwise have occurred. A whole stream of events issue from the decision, raising in one's favor all manner of unforeseen incidents and meetings and material assistance which no man could have dreamed could come his way."
>
> —William H. Murray

As you make the decision to step out in faith toward your dream, always look for God's hand and assistance in everything you do. He will be there. Look for Him and His providential work on your behalf, and remember that we *can do all things through Him who gives us strength.*

Sadly, many around you have chosen to live their fears instead of living their dreams. But you are different. You have chosen to not only dream, but to dream courageously. I salute you for pursuing your courageous dreams. So forever—Dream on . . . Dream until your dreams come true!

And may your journey be richly blessed.

Additional Readings

Shaping Your Thoughts

Acres of Diamonds, Russell Conwell

As a Man Thinketh, James Allen

Awaken the Giant Within, Anthony Robbins

Battlefield of the Mind, Joyce Meyer

How to Think Like Leonardo da Vinci, Michael Gelb

Learned Optimism, Martin E. Seligman

Prisoners of Our Thoughts, Alex Pattakos

Psycho-Cybernetics, Maxwell Maltz M.D.

Success Trough a Positive Mental Attitude, Napoleon Hill and W. Clement Stone

The Magic of Believing, Claude M. Bristol

The Magic of Thinking Big, David Schwartz, PhD

The Millionaire Mind, Thomas J. Stanley

The PowerMind System, Michael Monroe Kiefer

The Power of Positive Thinking, Norman Vincent Peale

The Power of Your Subconscious Mind, Joseph Murphy, PhD

Think and Grow Rich, Napoleon Hill

Thinking For A Change, John C. Maxwell

Thoughts are Things, Prentice Mulford

Your Best Life Now: 7 Steps to Living at Your Full Potential, Joel Osteen

The Bible, or your own religious book

Discovering Your Values, Strengths, Purpose, and Dreams

Built to Last, Jim Collins and Jerry Porras

Chicken Soup for the Soul: Living Your Dreams, Jack Canfield

Cure for the Common Life, Max Lucado

Go Put Your Strengths to Work, Marcus Buckingham

Goals! How to Get Everything You Want, Brian Tracy

If You Want to Walk on Water, You've Got to Get out of the Boat, John Ortberg

Living at the Summit, Dr. Tom Hill and Rebecca McDannold

Man's Search for Meaning, Viktor E. Frankl

Now, Discover Your Strengths, Marcus Buckingham and Donald O. Clifton

Soar with Your Strengths, Donald O. Clifton

StrengthsFinder 2.0, Tom Rath

The 7 Habits of Highly Effective People, Stephen R. Covey

The 8th Habit, Stephen R. Covey

The Dream Giver, Bruce Wilkinson

The Personality Code, Travis Bradberry

The Purpose Drive Life: What on Earth Am I Here For?, Rick Warren

Guides for Life Balance & Health

First Things First, Stephen R. Covey

The Corporate Athlete, Jack Croppel

The Power of Full Engagement, Jim Loehr and Tony Schwartz

The One Minute Manager Balances Work and Life, Ken Blanchard

You, The Owners Manual, Michael F. Roizen, M.D. and Mehmet C. Oz M.D.

Guides to Personal Success

Everyday Greatness, Stephen R. Covey

Get Out of Your Own Way, Robert K. Cooper, PhD

Good to Great, Jim Collins

How to Win Friends & Influence People, Dale Carnegie

Leadership and the New Science, Margaret Wheatley

Maximum Achievement, Brian Tracy

Rich Dad, Poor Dad, Robert T. Kiyosaki

Riches Within Your Reach, Robert Collier

See You at the Top, Zig Ziglar

Synchronicity, The Inner Path of Leadership, Joseph Jaworski

The Law of Success, Napoleon Hill

The Power of Focus, Jack Canfield

The Secret of the Ages, Robert Collier

The Science of Getting Rich, Wallace D. Wattles

The Science of Success, James Arthur Ray

The Strangest Secret, Earl Nightingale (audio)

The Success Principles, Jack Canfield

Index

About the Author

Ron Brown is an organizational effectiveness consultant and executive coach, serving corporations and leaders in both for-profit and not-for-profit organizations.

Ron specializes in helping clients implement creative solutions for a variety of organizational development needs, including leadership and executive development, employee engagement, strategic planning, continuous improvement initiatives, project management, organizational realignments, and leadership accountability. He also provides strategic coaching for individuals, sales teams, and emerging leaders. In addition, Ron serves as director of ministry & staff in Youth for Christ and is an adjunct professor of leadership studies at Greenville College, located in central Illinois.

Ron and his wife, Martha, live in Mahomet, Illinois, and have been married for twenty-three years and have three children. Ron serves his local community by being involved in its student-mentoring program and volunteering as a coach for the local high school football team.

Ron has a PhD in organizational leadership from Regent University, Virginia; both a bachelor's and master's degree in electrical engineering from the University of Illinois; and a master's in religion from Trinity International University in Deerfield, Illinois.

The *Courageous Life* Journal

As you process the contents of this book, use these pages to journal your Thoughts, Purpose, Goals, and Dreams.

* * *